disAPPOINTED:

Didn't I Say APPOINTED
Part I

Robert L. Crawford II

Copyright © 2018 by Robert L Crawford II

All rights reserved. In accordance with the U.S. Copyright Act of 1976, the scanning, uploading, and electronic sharing of any part of this book without the permission of the publisher is unlawful piracy and theft of the author's intellectual property.

If you would like to use material from the book (other than for review purposes), prior written permission must be obtained by contacting the publisher at permission@rlcrawford.org. Thank you for your support of the author's rights.

www.RLCrawford.org

Printed in the United States of America

ISBN #: 978-1-73216-490-1

This book is dedicated to **YOU**!

You have chosen to take the first step in no longer settling for mediocrity but excelling and walking in the power and authority given to you by Jesus Christ. I pray this book motivates you to look at your lessons and see the blessings. Remember when you feel disAPPOINTED, God says "Didn't I Say Appointed!"

Acknowledgments

I would like to express my humblest gratitude to the many people who saw me through this book; to all those who provided encouragement, was a listening ear, read, offered comments, allowed me to quote them, and assisted in the design. A few people who I would like to thank for helping make this dream a reality. Deedria Chauntee, words cannot express my gratitude for you! You are truly an angel in disguise! You are a real friend and a blessing in the lives of those you meet, #WeWin. Craig, bro you are a real life saver! You fought to defend my freedom #Marines, and then you were a listening ear and non-judgmental support in all my "plans." Pastor Sonya E. Williams, thank you for leading and nurturing my spirit. You saw the gift God gave me and pushed me towards it. I went kicking and fighting but you never gave up on me even in our disagreements. Thank you for your support and your prayers. Lakara Foster, thank you for the teaching that brought this work to fruition. Continue to minister in the way you do because you are truly anointed! My RIM Family, thank you all for being who you are I love each of you and appreciate your love and support. My MHD Family, thank you for daily asking how's the book coming and being more excited than me. Your enthusiasm kept me motivated! Special thanks to Mrs. Omalara!

> Last and not least: I beg forgiveness of all whose names I have failed to mention. Charge it to my head and not my heart, I love you and appreciate you none the less.

disAPPOINTED:

Didn't I Say APPOINTED

Part I

Robert L. Crawford II

Receive God's Overflow

"You let people ride over our heads; we went through fire and water, but you brought us to a place of abundance." (Psalm 66:12, NIV)

Regardless of what your circumstances and situations may seem, rest and be assured that God plans to bring you through to a place of more abundance. God desires for you to have an abundance of peace, an abundance of joy, an abundance of resources—He desires for you to overflow with His blessings so that you can be a blessing to the people who come in contact with you.

If you want to live in the overflow of God's blessings, you have to have an attitude to receive the overflow. Remember, as a believer in Jesus, you are a child of the Most High God. Royal blood is flowing through your veins. You were not created to be average. You were not created to get by and drag through life barely. You have tools of prominence on the inside. You are well equipped to do whatever God has called you to do!

Today, put your shoulders back, hold your head up high and start thinking like a victorious person. When you are a victor, you know that any adversity in your life is not permanent; it is temporary. Have the attitude to welcome in the overflow of God's abundance. Keep believing, trusting, and expecting because it is just a matter of time until He turns things around in your favor!

Say Continually

"To those who want the best for me, I wish them joy and happiness. May they always say, "Praise the Lord, who wants what is best for his servant." (Psalms 35:27 NRSV)

God's people were commanded to go around saying continually, "Let God be magnified and glorified. He takes pleasure in blessing me." I believe one of the reasons they were expected to say this continually is so it would get down on the inside of them. They would begin to believe and trust it after so many repetitions.

When we hear something long enough, we start to believe it. It starts to change the way we perceive things. What would happen if, just if, all throughout the day, we decided to stop dwelling on negative, defeated thoughts like, "I will never get out of debt. My business will never grow. I will never own a home. I will never get a good job. My children will never go to college." What if, just if, you started dwelling on thoughts like, "God enjoys blessing me! My blessings are on the way! My future is brighter than the eye can see! God has opened the windows of Heaven I am receiving my blessings!".

Let the certainty of God's Word descend into your heart. All throughout the day, declare His righteousness! His faithfulness! Declare that you are blessed by Him who continually loves to bless you!

Heavy with Favor

"Jerusalem, get up and shine! Your Light is coming! The Glory of the Lord will shine on you." (Isaiah 60:1, NRSV)

The Word did not say that the glory of the Lord is going to come on you one day. It did not say, "Maybe when the economy gets better, when you graduate from college, or when you get that good job, or that good boo or bae." It tells you that God's glory IS already on you!

The word "glory" in the Hebrew language indicates that God's favor, blessing, and splendor is on you in a heavy way. It is something that is tangible and has authority. Think about it like this: You are not less than, intimidated, scared, beneath, or frail; you are heavy with God's favor. You are overflowing with God's goodness. Your attitude and mindset should remain, there's no telling the greatness in my future! Yes, I am weighted down! However, it is not with burdens, problems, and the vicissitudes of life. I am weighed down with the favor of God!

When you truly understand that you are heavy with favor, then it is effortless to be even heavier with expectation. It is painless to believe for great things when you know God has favored you in a mighty way. It is time for you to rise! It is time for you to shine bright like a diamond! Let that manifest itself into your spirit today because this is your season because His grace, mercy, and favor are heavy upon you!

Gift of Forgiveness

"Don't judge others, and God will not judge you. Don't condemn others, and you will not be condemned. Forgive others, and you will be forgiven."
(Luke 6:37, NKJV)

The ability to forgive others is a true gift from God. The word tells us that if we do not forgive others, we cannot be forgiven. If we do not forgive, we are blocking the ability for God to work in our lives. When we choose to forgive others and ourselves, we are choosing God's way and allowing the door for Him to heal our hurts and restore us to His glory to open.

Now, forgiveness does not justify what that person or that you even have to get back into a "ship" with them (relationship, friendship, courtship, etc.). Forgiveness purely liberates the obligation owed to you so that God can discharge the debt owed to Him. Ask God to search your heart and show you if there is any unforgiveness blocking His blessing in your life. Ask Him to show you more about His gift of forgiveness so that you can walk in your true freedom and victory He has for you.

 A New Thing

"because I am doing something new! Now you will grow like a new plant. Surely you know this is true. I will even make a road in the desert, and rivers will flow through that dry land." (Isaiah 43:19, NLT)

Can you see the "new thing" God is doing in your life? Sometimes it is easy to see the hand of God moving, but let's be honest, sometimes the trials and tribulations of life can block our vision. No matter where you may be in life, meditate on His truth that God is working even when you cannot see or feel Him. When a seed is planted deep in the ground, it is surrounded by darkness and is alone. It is in those dark and alone times that life comes forth and begins to grow into something great. Trust and believe that God is doing a new thing in you and your life! You can trust Him because He is faithful! His plan for you is a blessing, to give you a future and a hope. He plans to do a new thing in your life and through your life. Let go of the thoughts of the past, we all have one, but the good news is we do not live there anymore. Now open your heart to what God is doing! Ask Him to show you what He is doing, to show it to your heart. Seek Him, and you will find Him and see the new thing He is doing in you!

A Different Spirit

"But my servant Caleb was different. He follows me completely. So I will bring him into the land that he has already seen, and his people will get that land." (Numbers 14:24, ERV)

One time in Scripture, Moses sent twelve men to spy out the Promised Land. The people of Israel were camped right next door and excited about taking ownership of the land. After 40 days, ten of the men sent into the land, came back with a negative report. They reported that there are giants in the land, and they could never defeat them." That negative report spread throughout the rest of the camp, and the people began to murmur and complain. However, Caleb said, "Moses, we are well able to defeat these people. Let us go up at once and take the land!"

It is thought-provoking that they all saw the same land, the same people, and the same circumstances; yet, they had completely different views. How could their reports be so contradictory? Here's how: Caleb had a different spirit. He has a different assessment. Others were focused on the the size of the people, but Caleb was focused on his bigger giant, God. The people who complained never actually made it into the Promised Land, but Caleb did. He accompanied a new generation that chose the blessing of God.

You have to choose to have that different spirit. Don't listen to what everyone else has to say; listen to what God says. Don't believe what others say about you, but believe what God has called you. Don't put your trust in man, but put your trust in the one who made the man. Don't fear the giants, but know you have a bigger giant in your team. Choose to believe, trust, obey Him, and His perspective and He will lead you into your promised land!

Shut the Door on Fear

"Don't give the devil a way to defeat you." (Ephesians 4:27, ISV)

So many people are living with less than God's best because they have allowed fear to creep in and take root in their lives. Fear is the greatest weapon the adversary uses to try to hold us back. Fear is not from God. Scripture tells us that fear brings torment; it is designed to paralyze us and keep us from God's blessings. Here is the good news: our God is greater than that fear. His power in you is greater than any power that comes against you. To walk in His power, you have to close the door on the enemy, slam it shut with authority. See, the enemy cannot have access to your life unless you open a door and give him access. Remember, life and death lie in the power of your tongue. When we open ourselves to fear, we give the enemy opportunity.

If you have allowed fear to steal from you in any area of life, you can be unrestricted — you can be finished with fear. Conquering the enemy starts by choosing to close the door on fear by receiving God's love and meditating on His promises. Receive His truth and speak His truth. Let Him set you free and lead you to victory.

Strength and Joy

"He lives in the presence of glory and honor. His Temple is a place of power and joy." (1st Chronicles 16:27 ERV)

Do you desire more strength and joy in your life? The Word of God tells us that in God's presence, there is the fullness of joy — the most abundant and absolute! When you have God's joy, you take on His supernatural strength. There's nothing that can come against you or stop you when you are filled with the strength and joy of the Lord. "No weapon formed against me shall work" (Isaiah.54:17 NRSV)

Notice this verse specifically says that strength and joy are found in His sanctuary. One translation says they are found "where He is." Do you know "where He is?" The Spirit of the Almighty is alive in every believer. It also says that He inhabits the praises of His people. That means when you begin to praise and worship God, either corporately in a church setting or privately in your personal time, God's presence is there. You are His sanctuary, and when we worship together, God shows up in a special way.

Anytime you are feeling depleted or overwhelmed by circumstances or situations of life, just go into a fit of praise. Begin to declare His goodness and faithfulness to you. He'll fill you with His joy and strength because in His presence is where that's found! Stay strong and remember the joy you have, the world didn't give it, and the world can't take it away.

I Refuse to Worry

"Can anyone of you by worrying add a single hour to your life?"
(Matthew 6:27 NRSV)

God doesn't want you to live worried and anxious about anything! He knows that worry is counterproductive to His will. It steals your peace and joy and affects every area of your life, even your sleep! My grandmother would tell me, "You gonna worry yourself sick?" Yes, worrying will make you physically ill. You never gain anything by worrying; in fact, it causes you to lose precious moments that you can never get back. The good news is, God has promised to give you victory over worry. When you choose to put down worry, you pick up God's peace.

Decide immediately to put an end to worry. Don't feed worry by focusing on the negative and false news all the time. Sure, we should be informed, but we should be more informed of the truth through the Word of God. Feed your faith and fill your heart and mind with God's promises. Declare every day, "My God shall supply ALL my needs. He makes a way out of no way. He is a Restorer and Redeemer." Focus on God's Word; you'll drive out worry and fill your heart with faith and expectancy for the future! He is Jehovah Shalom (The Lord our Peace).

If it's meant to be, it's up to YOU!!!!

"Be joyful in hope, Patient in affliction, faithful in prayer"
(Romans 12:12 NIV)

We are all human living in a world of uncertainties and unknowns. We make plans, and in the middle of our plans, life happens. Even when it seems like we are at the end of our rope or our backs are against the wall, we still can WIN! With God, the possibilities are limitless. It is up to us to Trust in HIM, Believe in HIM, and Depend on HIM.

How do we do that? Through your praise, your press, and your prayer. Praise- Your anyhow praise. When you can't see it, praise Him anyhow. Your praise is your weapon. Your praise is the transportation to get you through.

Press- Embrace your struggle. Not enjoy your struggle, no pity parties. While you are going through, learn what you need to get out of this situation. Fighting when you want to give up strengthens your mental muscles.

Pray- Pray without ceasing. For your situation to change, you must first be changed. Notice the maturity of your prayers when you are going through. Intercede for others while you are praying for yourself.

Think of it like this. God is the bank. He has given you the debit card. Praise gives you the direction to the ATM. Press is what gets you to the ATM. Prayer is the PIN number! Go to the bank today!!

Elevate the Ordinary

"Remind your people that they should always be under the authority of rulers and government leaders. They should obey these leaders and be ready to do good." (Titus 3:1, ERV)

Question: How do you honor God? Many times people think, "I go to church to honor God, or I read the Bible, sing and clap my hands in praise and worship to honor God." Is one of those or something similar how you honor God? Those are ways to honor God, yes, but did you know that you also honor God when you get to work or arrive at church on time? You honor God when you are productive each day and respect the people who are in authority over you. You honor God when you excel at your job or in school.

Actions speak louder than words; we've all heard that countless times in life. When you give your very best in the workplace, your whole life is giving praise to God. Showing up with an upright attitude, being hospitable, organized, being and bringing your best — people will notice there's something different about you, they'll want what you have.

As followers of Christ and believers in His Word, we have to set the standard in all areas of life. People should see the depth of your character and your spirit of excellence and know that you are a child of the Most High God. Decide to honor Him in all that you do because you are His representative, His hands, and feet in the earth.

In All Situations

"But we belong to the day, so we should control ourselves. We should wear faith and love to protect us. And the hope of salvation should be our helmet."
(1 Thessalonians 5:18, ERV)

Are you giving thanks in every circumstance? No matter if it is good, bad, or ugly? This might seem like a stretch to start, especially when you are going through the trials and tribulations of life. Notice the scripture does not say to give thanks "for" everything; it says give thanks "in" everything. This means, no matter what's going on, no matter how bad or dismal it may seem, find something to be thankful for. Don't just focus on what's wrong in your life; focus on what's good and what God is currently, and going to do in your life.

When you are grateful, it opens the door for God to begin to move on your behalf. That's why it says "this is God's will for you," not this might be or could be God's will for you. He wants you to be close to Him to accept His strength and power by giving thanks. That's why we should maintain the attitude that says, "God, regardless of what happened, I will to be grateful. Sickness may plague my body, but that's when I know you to be Jehovah Rapha. Thank you for trial and tribulations, that's when you are Jehovah Shalom. As you give thanks for any and everything, you will see God's hand move mightily on your behalf, and you'll come out of that difficulty improved, tougher and wiser than before.

Trust His Timing

"My life is in your hands. Save me from those who are persecuting me." (Psalm 31:15, ERV)

God doesn't always work according to our schedule or in our time. In a single moment, the twinkling of an eye, God can change your entire life! All throughout scripture, we see examples of how God was working behind the scenes and instantly turned things around for His people. Scripture tells us He is the same yesterday, today and forever more, which means if He did it before, He could do it again. He can instantly turn things around for you!

You may be going through some ups and downs today, but stay encouraged because your times are in God's hands. Trust that He has your best interest at heart, and all things are working for your good. He wants to pour out His favor and take you further than you could dream possible. He wants to work in your life in ways beyond what you have ever imagined.

Let this truth settle deep down into your soul. Resist discouragement by speaking His Word over your life, present, and future. Keep standing, keep hoping, and keep believing because He is working behind the scenes. Have faith and trust because your times are in His hands, and He will lead you in the life of victory He has destined for you!

# So Be It

"For no matter how many promises God has made, they are "Yes" in Christ. And so through him, the "Amen" is spoken by us to the glory of God."
(2 Corinthians 1:20, NRSV)

Have you considered and acknowledged the fact that God has already said "yes" to His promises concerning life? You don't have to beg God to bless you. You don't have to plead and bargain with Him to help you in your times of need. God desires to be there for you. He wants you to see that He is able to do exceedingly and abundantly above all you could ask or even think!

The Word tells us His promises are "yes and amen." The translation of Amen is "so be it." In other words, it's already done its signed, sealed, delivered, approved, and cleared. All you have to do is make sure you are doing your part. God's love is absolute, but there is a stipulation, we have to obey His commands to see His promises come to fruition. For example, Malachi 3:10 (NIV) states "Bring the whole tithe into the storehouse, that there may be food in my house. Test me in this," says the Lord Almighty, "and see if I will not throw open the floodgates of heaven and pour out so much blessing that there will not be room enough to store it."

We have to bring our tithe to Him to see the windows of heaven open and blessings to flow upon our lives. The good news is that when we surrender our hearts to Him, He empowers us to fulfill every one of His commands. He equips us for every good work because He wants to see us live a blessed and abundant life! This is why His promises are simply "yes" and "amen"!

The Good Outweighs the Bad

"But thanks be to God, who always leads us as captives in Christ's triumphal procession and uses us to spread the aroma of the knowledge of him everywhere."
(2 Corinthians 2:14, NKJV)

Think about your past, what events or occasions do you remember? What memories do you allow to play on repeat in your mind? In the Old Testament, they had what they called memorial stones. These were used to remind the people about the good things God did in their lives — their victories. We have to remind ourselves to focus more on our victories, as well.

Sure, we have all had setbacks, but when you meditate on your disappointments and failures, it only drains you of energy and places a negative cloud over everything that could be seen good. It steals your confidence, trust, joy, and even your faith. But when you change and focus on your victories, it builds your strength, endurance, trust, and confidence. It feeds and increases your faith! It gives you a reason to give God all glory, honor, and praise!

I enliven you today to get into the habit of focusing more on your victories. Remember, every good and perfect gift comes from Him! As you praise and thank Him for His favor and victory in your life, He'll pour out His blessings on you. He'll open and put His super on natural doors for you to move forward in strength to fulfill the dreams and desires He has placed in your heart!

Sooner Than Later

"So do not throw away your confidence; it will be richly rewarded."
(Hebrews 10:35, NIV)

Have you been praying, trusting, and believing in something from God, and it seems like it's taking a lot longer than you thought to come to fruition? Many times, people can miss God's best simply because they give up before their time. Don't let that be you! Be encouraged today, your answer and blessing are a lot closer than you think. If it seems like things are getting harder or worse than it started, remember, when the storm is at its worse, which means you are closer to your blessing. Weeping may endure for a night, BUT joy comes in the morning light.

We serve a faithful God, and He is always working behind the scenes on your behalf. Don't cast away your confidence; your reward is coming! Just like a mother forgets about her labor pain when she is holding her newborn baby, you'll forget about your struggle when you are holding on to your blessings. However, while you are in the holding pattern, keep an attitude of faith and expectancy. When you open your eyes, every morning and speak over yourself, "He's brought me, and I have come too far to give up now! This is my season, and I will reap my bountiful harvest." Stand firm in faith and look for His hand of blessing because He has promised you victory, and it's a lot closer than you think!

is Gifts

"Do not boast about tomorrow, for you do not know what a day may bring."
(Proverbs 27:1, AMP)

Question: Do you see every day and its ups and downs as a blessed gift from God? Many times when asked this, we may be tempted to brush it off and say, "Yeah, yeah, I know. This is the day that the Lord has made." But truly it is! God ordained, meaning He created it and all its complexities, before the foundation of the earth. He has already ordered an abundance blessings just for you. He has already orchestrated the right opportunities to cross your path. He has already made the right connections and partnerships for you. In addition to that, the air you inhale and exhale, the food you eat, whether you like it or not, even the sun kissing you on your face are all part of the great blessing that God gives every single day.

Remember, tomorrow is not promised, so don't waste a single moment living life defeated and depressed! Our attitude should not be, "I have to take care of the kids," or "I have to go to work." It should be, "I get to take care of the kids God has blessed me with," or "I get to go out and do the job God has blessed me with to get me to my next destination." Acknowledge every opportunity as a gift from God wrapped with a beautiful bow. Count your blessings, small and big, then watch Him multiply them exceedingly all the days of your life!

Fully Accept His Yes

"For as many are the promises of God, in Christ, they are [all answered] "Yes." So through Him, we say our "Amen" to the glory of God."
(2 Corinthians 1:20, AMP)

When God laid out the blueprint that was to become your life, He placed the correct people, the precise breaks, and the accurate open doors. In other words, He already had your "yeses" planned out — Yes, you can and will accomplish your dreams! Yes, you can overcome that obstacle! Yes, you can open that business! Yes, you can be successful and succeed! His YES is in your future!

The question remains, will you fully and undoubtedly say "yes" to God's "yes"? Are you going to double dog dare to believe Him — to get into agreement with His promises?

Start right now by professing and proclaiming His promises over your life. Start declaring that He is great and all-powerful and that His plan will come to pass on your behalf. Don't let doubt and discouragement distract you, but keep your eyes fixed on Him because He is not like man and He cannot lie. His promises are always yes and amen. So fully accept His "yes"!

Over and Over Again

"Ask and keep on asking, and it will be given to you; seek and keep on seeking, and you will find; knock and keep on knocking, and the door will be opened for you." (Matthew 7:7, NLT)

Sometimes, people get discouraged in life because things didn't turn out the way they hoped initially. It could be they put so much energy into a relationship, that just didn't work out. They attempted that new business venture, yet they are still struggling with their finances. Now they begin to think it's never going to happen for them. But, one thing we have to learn to remember and hold as truth is that God honors perseverance! On the way to your "yes" you may come across a lot of "no's." You may find a lot of closed doors, but that doesn't mean the final answer is denied. It just means just keep swimming, swimming, swimming, just keep going and try again.

If God promised it, He is going to bring it to pass. The Word tells us that through faith and patience we inherit God's promises. It's in the "no" season or the shut door season, that patience comes in; this is where perseverance and trust come in. Just because you don't see things happen right away doesn't mean you should quit. No, instead, rise and press forward. Keep believing, keep hoping, keep enduring, keep pressing, and keep asking because our God is ALWAYS faithful to His word!

Do a Double Take

"Then Elijah said to his servant, "Go up higher and look toward the sea." The servant went and looked. He came back and said, "I saw nothing." Elijah told him to look again. This happened seven times. The seventh time, the servant came back and said, "I saw a small cloud the size of a man's fist that was coming in from the sea." Elijah told the servant, "Go tell King Ahab to get his chariot ready and go home now. If he does not leave now, the rain will stop him." (1 Kings 18:43–44, ERV)

The Word says that after the prophet Elijah prayed asking God to end the drought, he said to the people, "I can hear the sound of rain." He was essentially saying, "There is a yes from God in our future!" Elijah instructed his assistant to look towards the sea to check if there was any sign, big or small of rain. When he came back, he said, "No, Elijah. There's not a single cloud in the sky. It's clear." Elijah didn't get discouraged and think, "What are we going to do now? I told the people there will be rain." Instead, he simply said, "Go back and look again." In my mind, it was a do a double take just to be sure you saw what you think you saw.

This happened not one, two, or even three times, but six different times and Elijah kept saying, "Go look again." On the seventh time, God's number of completion, he came back, but this time his response was different. This time he said, *"I saw a small cloud the size of a man's fist that was coming in from the sea."* Elijah's answer was basically, "It's gonna rain on your head!" Like Elijah, maybe you believe in something and aren't seeing anything happen to make it happen. Don't give up, go back and look a second, third, or forth time. Just keep looking until you see God moving! If God has promised it, He will do it. It won't be long until you see a small cloud the size of a man's fist bringing forth your showers of blessings in every area of your life. Remember you have to see it before you see it, or you never will see it.

There Remaineth a Rest

"For we who have believed do enter into that rest; even as he hath said, as I swore in my wrath, They shall not enter into my rest: although the works were finished from the foundation of the world." (Hebrews 4:3, ASV)

God promises that there are set things in our future, but He doesn't tell us when they will happen. Your time may be tomorrow morning at 1:34. You'll get the call, text, or email; you've been waiting for. Your time may be two years from now when you get that favor that will propel you to a new level in life. The question is, "Do you trust God enough to believe that your times are coming?" Are you willing to wait with a grateful attitude? Are you willing to get His perspective?

The time is already set in your future. Don't let the negative thoughts and people talk you out of it. The way you know that you're believing is that you have joy and rest on the inside. You're at the place of peace that surpasses all understanding. You know His answer is on the way and you trust that God is working things out for you and in your favor. Your time of favor is on the way!

Through Faith and Patience

"We don't want you to be lazy. We want you to be like those who, because of their faith and patience, will get what God has promised." (Hebrews 6:12, ERV)

In today's culture, people are use to getting things instantly. We've been programmed for immediacy. People despise having to wait. The Word tells us, "It's through faith and patience that we inherit God's promises." Sometimes in life, it is rather easy for people to have faith. We declare, "God, I believe I'm going to accomplish all my dreams. God, I believe I'm going to overcome this obstacle in my life." It gets harder when we have to exercise patience.

Our prayer should be "God, I trust you, your will, your way, and your timing. I shall not get discouraged or give up because I know it's all working for my good. I will wait with faith and patience because I know it shall come to pass! In Jesus name, Amen." Through faith and patience, we inherit His promises. Trust His Word, trust His timing, and trust that your answer is on its way!

Be still and Know

"God says, "Stop fighting and know that I am God! I am the one who defeats the nations; I am the one who controls the world." (Psalm 46:10, NIV)

Most people are used to having constant activity: computers, cell phones, television, email, video games, etc. There's nothing wrong with any of that, that is our culture, but the Word tells us that we need to be still so we can concentrate on knowing God. I've found this to be true especially during the trials and tribulations of life. When you are faced with a challenge, it's easy to want to run to a family member, good friend or co-worker, but at some points, you have to stop and say, "God, I rest in You. I know You have me in the palm of Your hand."

Our battles are not with flesh and blood, but with principalities of evil. The people in your life aren't the source of your problems, we battle the principalities, powers, and rulers of the darkness of the world. Be still and know that God, the Alpha and Omega, the beginning and the end, resides inside of you, you are putting yourself in a position of strength and authority. Take time to stop, and just be still in His presence. Let His peace reign over you. Let Him refresh you by His Spirit. Remember, this battle is not yours; it's the Lords. Be still before Him so you can know His hand of victory in every area of your life!

Enter with This

"Enter into his gates with thanksgiving, And into his courts with praise: Give thanks unto him, and bless his name." (Psalm 100:4, NKJV)

As followers of Christ, we have the honor and privilege to enter boldly into God's presence with our heads held high. The Word says that we can come to His throne of grace and receive His mercy because He loves us, we have unlimited access to Him 24 hours a day, seven days a week, 365 days a year (366 on leap year). Today's verse tells us that we shouldn't just come any type way to God. We shouldn't come empty-handed to the throne. So you ask what can I bring? What do I have that's worthy of God? The answer is simple: Your praise, thanksgiving, and worship. Always enter His gates with an offering from your heart of adoration because He is worthy!

We have to understand; praise isn't just about singing songs on Sunday mornings. Praise is the expression of gratefulness to Father God for Who He is and all that He has done. Praise gets God's attention. Praise is a powerful tool in the life of the believer because God inhabits the praise of His people! When we enter His presence the right way, He enters our circumstances, and when God shows up, the enemy has no choice but to retreat! Today, enter into His gates with thanksgiving and open the door for Him to move on your behalf!

Wines on the Way

"But thanks be to God, who always leads us as captives in Christ's triumphal procession and uses us to spread the aroma of the knowledge of him everywhere." (2 Corinthians 2:14, NIV)

Isn't it wonderful and brings a sense of peace to stand on the promise that God will always lead us to victory? That means no matter what is going on in your life today, no matter what's happening in the world around you, no matter what anybody says, you should always be thanking God because your victory is on the way to your situation!

You don't have to wait for everything to be perfect before you decide to celebrate what God is going to do in your life. Praise is putting action behind your faith. In the middle of adversity or a tough time, start making a list of who you're going to invite to your celebration party versus a pity party. That means if you're in the hospital, start planning what you're going to do when you get out. If you lost your job, start planning your new employment party. When things don't look favorable in the natural, remember, we serve a SUPERnatural God. With God as your leader victory is yours, always expect an increase. You can plan for restoration. You can plan for a comeback, and you can plan for victory because He is leading and guiding you in Jesus' name!

The Power of Ignore

"But some scoundrels said, 'How can this fellow save us?' They despised him and brought him no gifts. But Saul kept silent." (1 Samuel 10:27, NIV)

In the Word, King Saul had some people come against him; he had some haters. They were bullying him for whatever their reasoning was. Saul could have easily become distracted and lost his focus on what he was supposed to be doing. He could stop to their level and defended himself saying, "I'm a good leader. I have what it takes." But what did he do? He kept silent.

Sometimes that's what you have to do when people are coming to you. You have to realize that some people are just jealous, they envious of you for whatever their reason, and that is not yours to manage. Not everyone is going to have your best interest at heart, nor do they want to see you succeed and be the great person God has destined for you to be. Don't let them control your peace, joy, and not your destiny. Don't let them distract you from God's best intentions for you.

Instead of playing up to people or trying to win over all your critics, keep your eyes focused on what God has for you. Spend time with people who see what God is doing in you, for you, and through you. Focus on those who will celebrate you, ignore the haters so you can be all that God has called you to be.

You're in Good Company

"...but Jesus refused to answer." (Luke 23:9, NLT)

Many times people would attack Jesus and criticize Him. Many times it says, "Jesus answered them not a word." He simply didn't respond to His naysayers. He didn't try to convince them to change their minds. He didn't get upset because somebody didn't speak to him or was talking about Him. No, He just ignored it and remained silent.

When people attack you they're jealous, trying to make you look bad, trying to discourage you, remember you're in God's company! Jesus was probably criticized more than anyone else in the Bible. I admire how He never tried to explain himself. He didn't try to force everyone to understand and accepts Him. He just stayed focused on what He was called and ordained to do. He simply continued to run His race to see what the end would be.

Jesus set and was the example for us. We don't have to try to win the approval and favor of others. We have to understand that not everyone is going to understand us. Our focus should be on following God and letting Him direct our paths. The next time someone criticizes you, remember the example of Jesus. Overlook it, don't get offended, and keep moving forward in the destiny God has for you!

 Your Race

"Therefore, since we are surrounded by such a great cloud of witnesses, let us throw off everything that hinders and the sin that so easily entangles. And let us run with perseverance the race marked out for us, fixing our eyes on Jesus, the pioneer, and perfecter of faith. For the joy set before him, he endured the cross, scorning its shame, and sat down at the right hand of the throne of God" (Hebrews 12:1–2, NKJV)

It's effortless to be tempted to go through life in competition with everyone. When we see someone who's more talented, better looking or has more gifts, instead of staying in our lane and being comfortable with who we are, often we feel inferior and think, "I've got to catch up or be better than them." The problem with this unhealthy competition is that it's a never-ending cycle.

There will always be someone bigger and worse, as my mother would say. It's a very freeing thing when you realize, you don't have to compete with anyone. I don't have to have as big a house as my neighbor to feel good about myself. I don't have to keep up with my co-worker. I don't have to be a certain size. No, I understand that I'm not in competition with my friend, my neighbor or my co-worker. Instead, I'm going to be the best me that I can be. That is the type of attitude, God prefers to work with. When you focus on being who God made you be, that's when you'll rise higher and position yourself for every spiritual blessing He has in store for you!

et God Arise

"Let God arise, let His enemies be scattered..." (Psalm 68:1, NKJV)

What are you letting arise in your life? In layman terms, what are you focusing your words, energy, and thoughts on? You might say, "Times are just so hard right now, or I've lost some money." "My health doesn't look good. My boo just walked out on me." Stop, you're focusing on the wrong things. You're letting defeat, discouragement, and self-pity rise up. Why not turn that around and say, "God is still in control. Somebody may have walked out on me, I may be hurting right now, but I know God is the Restorer of my soul and the center of my joy." "I may have lost money, but I'm not worried I know my God is my source and money is just a resource. He is supplying all of my needs, and He is and will fight all my battles."

When you start giving God glory and letting Him arise in your life, you can't stay defeated. Your enemies will be scattered! They'll tremble at your words of faith. Start now by declaring God's goodness in your life and let Him arise so that you can move forward in the victory He has for you!

Promotion comes from the Lord

"For not from the east nor from the west nor from the south come promotion and lifting up. But God is the Judge! He puts down one and lifts up another." (Psalm 75:6–7, AMP)

Have you ever noticed that people tend to act differently around those they think can benefit from— people who appear to have status, wealth or influence in life? I believe that the way we treat people is a test. I believe God will bring people into your life that may seem insignificant to you right now. They may not appear to be able to benefit you, but in reality, they are divinely linked to your destiny. They hold the key to your promotion and increase. Will you treat them with respect and honor even if you think they can't do anything for you?

The truth is that the people we're playing up to or trying to win their favor may be the ones that open a door for us, but they don't hold the key to your destiny. Promotion doesn't come from them; promotion comes from God and God alone. God can and will use the most unlikely people to open doors of opportunity for you — a security guard, greeter at Wal-Mart, even a homeless individual. Let's pass the test and treat everyone like Jesus put them in our path because He probably did. Show hospitality to strangers, by so doing some people have shown hospitality to angels without knowing it.

The Trail of Preparation

"In their hearts, humans plan their course, but the Lord establishes their steps." (Proverbs 16:9, NIV)

You have heard the analogy you have to pass this test before you can take on the next. God will often use our experiences of life as stepping stones in preparation for what He has in store next for us. The Word tells us that He'll even take the things the enemy tries to attack us with, turn them around, then use them for our good. He is always leading us on the trail of preparation.

This is why it is imperative to keep our eyes stayed on Him. We have to trust that when we submit to Him — even if we don't see or understand — He is still ordering all of our steps. If something is not happening in the time you want it to happen, remind yourself, God knows what He is doing. He has your best interest in His heart. God is preparing you. While waiting, don't make the mistake of trying to figure everything out. If you're constantly trying to figure things out, that will only frustrate you, if you are going to pray about it don't worry about it. Turn it over to God and declare, "God, I put my life and time in your hand. I cannot, will not, and shall not worry because I trust You. I know You are leading me on a journey of preparation for all the wonderful blessings You have in store for me."

Divine Appointments

"So my heart and soul will be very happy. Even my body will live in safety," (Proverbs 16:9, ERV)

There are some individuals that God has allowed to cross paths with your life to help you reach your purpose and destiny. They may not even know you, but they may introduce you to someone or put in a good word for you with someone you need to be connected with. They may have the wisdom or advice that will propel you towards your destiny. We have to remember that these divine appointments have been orchestrated by The Most High. Divine appointments aren't always the people you would expect to bring benefit to your life. In fact, usually, they are the people you don't expect — a clerk at the grocery store, a co-worker at the office, the homeless persons asking for change, someone who may just seem to be less influential.

God can give anyone an idea and use anyone to make a connection. Remember, He doesn't choose the equipped but equip the chosen. Never judge the message by the messenger, you never know who may have a word from God for you. We should always treat everyone we encounter with dignity, honor, and respect. You never know who God is going to use in your life. So be open, loving, kind, and sow good seeds that will open the doors to His divine appointments!

Your Constant Help

"God is our refuge and strength, an ever-present help in trouble."
(Psalm 46:1, NIV)

God is always with you, in your good doings, your bad doings, and even in your, you know you wrong doings, He is always with you. That means He is present at all times, continually, perpetually, throughout all existence. In your times of trial and tribulation, He promises to be a constant help. How is He your help? "Help" means something different to everybody, but help is defined as make it easier for (someone) to do something by offering one's services or resources. That's because "help" is specific to you and your specific need. If you needed money to pay your bills, what good would receiving a slice of chocolate cake do for you! He always knows exactly what you need and is always ready to provide it!

Are you facing trouble or adversity? Know that God is always with you. Look to Him, the source and not the resource, for your help. Trust that He has the answer and that He is working things out for you and all in your favor. While you continue believing Him and follow His direction, He will lead you in the way that you should go. He will comfort you, revive you, restore you and bless you! He will be your constant help because He is forever faithful to His Word!

True Comfort

"As a mother comforts her child, so will I comfort you; and you will be comforted over Jerusalem." (Isaiah 66:13, NIV)

A lot of times when people face difficult situations, their natural tendency is to seek comfort in things that are familiar with. It may range from work, an activity, family members, friends, working out, or food. These things may bring comfort, but it is only temporary comfort. Authentic comfort is found in a true relationship with Jesus.

According to Merriam-Webster, comfort is defined as to give strength and hope; to ease grief or trouble. No matter what hardship you may be facing, God desires to give you comfort. Just as a mother cares for her child, God longs to give you strength, hope, peace, and confidence. Open your heart, mind, and soul, turn to Him and receive His love. Let go of things that hold you back and down. Let Him heal your heart and give you strength for your future. Let Him empower you to rise and overcome every obstacle in Jesus name!

Ultimate Victory

"These things I have spoken unto you, that in me ye might have peace. In the world ye shall have tribulation: but be of good cheer; I have overcome the world." (John 16:33, KJV)

When trials and tribulations come, it is so easy to feel overwhelmed and get discouraged. You may feel lost or uncertain about your future and the ability to overcome what you presently see. That's exactly when we need to turn our hearts and minds to God because He has promised that no matter what we face, we can have His perfect peace. We can feel His agape love and have confidence, remember He has already overcome the world!

The key is that we have to keep our minds with an eternal perspective. We have to know this too shall pass, meaning that the trials that come are only temporary. We may experience tragedy or loss in this life, but with God on our side, we have the ultimate victory in eternity. We may have seasons of grief or sadness here on earth, but He is our comforter, and in the end, He will wipe away every tear from our eyes. Weeping may endure for a night, but Joy cometh……

Remember, when difficulties arise, focus on the fact that you have the ultimate victory. Don't let fear paralyze you; instead, put your faith and hope in God. Those things that the enemy meant for evil, God will turn around for your good. He'll lead you out stronger, wiser and more alive than ever before.

Whosoever

"Yes, God loved the world so much that he gave his only Son, so that everyone who believes in him would not be lost but have eternal life."
(John 3:16 ERV)

When God sent His only begotten Son down to earth, He opened the door of salvation to whoever would believe and accept His Son as their Lord and Savior. That means anyone: Black, white, Hispanic, Asian, straight, gay, tall, short, skinny, curvy; anyone can become a child of His and have everlasting life! Isn't it a relief that contrary to popular beliefs, He didn't just come to save certain kinds of people? Aren't you glad He doesn't have criteria or type for salvation?

Before Jesus came, people had to observe many laws to be considered holy enough to go into God's temple. When Jesus came, He was the ultimate and final sacrifice! His blood doesn't just cover our sins; it cleanses us and washes them away! Now, instead of going to the temple to be near God, the Word says we are the temple, and He lives inside of us.
Thank God for the gift of salvation to whosoever believes in Him. Walk and live in your truth and freedom, know if you love God, God Loves you also.

ile It Away

"Lord, my heart is not haughty, nor my eyes lofty. Neither do I concern me with great matters, nor with things too profound for me."
(Psalm 131:1, NKJV)

Have things ever happened that you did not plan for and you find yourself trying to figure it out or tuck it away in your mind so as not to think about it? What do you do when you can't make sense of it?

I'm glad you asked, the answer: We all need to create a file in our mind called the "Give it to God" file. When things come up that don't make sense, things that you can't figure out, instead of getting frustrated or confused, put it in your "Give it to God" file and leave it alone. If you go through life trying to figure out why something happened or why things just didn't work out, you will find yourself bitter, depressed, and going in circles around that same situation in life. Part of trusting God means trusting Him when you can't see the outcome or know the full plan; we know that His plan is always for our good. We have to know that He will reveal all things to us in His time.

Are there some things that have happened that you still can't understand or figure out? Things that you keep thinking on over and over and over in your mind. Those are the things you need to file away? Choose to trust God and keep moving forward. He loves you, He is for you, and He has a great plan for your future!

es You Can

"I can do all this through him who gives me strength."
(Philippians 4:13, NIV)

When was the last time you told yourself "Yes I can" with confidence? It's not something you think to do daily. Most people tend to magnify and focus solely on their limitations. It's easier to focus on your inadequacies than your possibilities. The Word makes it very simple: all things is possible to those who believe in Christ. It is possible to see all your dreams come to fruition. It is possible to overcome that obstacle that has plagued you for some time. Rise above your current situation, go to new heights and embrace your destiny.

You may not have worked out a plan, you may not know the time or the place, but you can rest assured that if God said you can then YES YOU CAN!

Anytime you have a moment repeat this verse to yourself again, say it to yourself aloud. Let it sink down deep into the fiber of your being. As you do, His word will begin to transform you, faith will rise up in your heart and will boldly embrace the blessings that He has in store for you!

Let your faith speak

"And since we have the same spirit of faith, according to what is written, 'I believed, and therefore I spoke,' we also believe and therefore speak."
(2 Corinthians 4:13, NRSV)

Every believer in Christ has been given a measure of faith. For you to see the promises of God in your life, you have to give your faith a voice. You have to declare what God says about you and your life in His Word. Those seeds of faith inside you are activated when you speak them out into the atmosphere. That's why the Word tells us, "Let the weak say I am strong. Let the poor say I am rich." When you let your faith speak it sends forth the Word of God, the Word says that He watches over His Word to bring it to pass in your life.

Every word you speak is a seed. Don't kill your seed by speaking against your faith! Don't allow words of defeat or negativity come out of your mouth, or someone else speaks them do not receive them into your spirit. Instead, water your seed by continuing to declare over it the Word of God. When you wake up every morning, thank Him that His promises are coming to fruition in your life. As you do, you will see those things come to pass and live the victorious life God has prepared for you!

Strong against Difficulty

"So do not fear, for I am with you; do not be dismayed, for I am your God. I will strengthen you and help you; I will uphold you with my righteous right hand." (Isaiah 41:10, NIV)

It's easy to look around at what's happening in the world today and feel concerned or dismayed. Circumstances, at times, may seem overwhelming. Maybe your business is struggling; you lost your job, you're struggling in a relationship, or concerned about the state of the government and the economy. It is during times like these; it's imperative to remember that God has promised that He will never leave us nor forsake us. The truth of the matter is, He is not only with us, But He has also promised to strengthen us and harden us to the difficulties of life. That means, when the storms start raging in your life, God raises that standard. Don't allow your temporary circumstances to steal your permanent joy and peace. Keep the attitude "This problem may be big, but the God I serve is bigger!"

Remember the enemy doesn't want your money; he's ultimately after your joy, peace, and testimony. He knows that if he can take your joy, then he can take your strength. When you stay connected to the Father through prayer, studying, and declaring His promises over your life, you'll be strengthened and enabled to endure difficulties and stay safe in the palm of God's hand!

Surprise

"If you fully obey the Lord your God and carefully follow all his commands I give you today, the Lord your God will set you high above all the nations on earth. All these blessings will come on you and accompany you if you obey the Lord your God:" (Deuteronomy 28:1–2, NIV)

A surprise is basically something that you weren't really expecting. It's something that can make you feel special and lets you know that someone is thinking about you. Surprises bring us joy and lift our spirits and hearts. God wants to surprise you and overwhelm you with His grace, mercy, and goodness. He wants to do things that make life easier and shows you just how much He loves you.

The word "overwhelm" can also be translated as "to catch by surprise." He wants to help you accomplish all of your dreams and aspirations, and overcome any obstacles you may face. He wants to blow your mind with His goodness and mercy.

Empty out your heart and mind, now fill it with what God wants to do in your life today. Maintain an attitude of faith and expectancy in spite of what you may face or be facing. Do this and see and receive the many surprises that God has with your name on it.

Do This for Your Health!

"Peace of mind makes the body healthy, but jealousy is like a cancer." (Proverbs 14:30, NIV)

How easy is it to let the pressures and distractions of life pull our thoughts away from God? Very easy! Within a second we stop focusing on God and get so focused on things that we feel overwhelmed and stressed out about. We weren't created to live anxious and worrisome life; we were meant to live in His total peace.

Did you know the best thing you can do for your health is to set your heart at peace with God? Peace isn't just a feeling; it's a powerful position. Peace means "to set back at one again." We can be settled in our minds and hearts when we are in alignment with God's Word. Being in alignment with God places you in a position of life, strength, and confidence!

Choose to keep your heart at peace by staying focused on God. Give life to your body by staying in agreement with Him, His Word, and His purpose for your life. Let God's peace guard your heart so that you can be equipped to live the abundant life He has promised to you!

Blessed Before Birth

"Before I made you in your mother's womb, I knew you. Before you were born, I chose you for special work. I chose you to be a prophet to the nations." (Jeremiah 1:5, ERV)

Did you know that God had plans for you before you were even born, even before your parents were born? He knew everything about you, your good, bad, ugly, and indifferent, way before you were placed in your mother's womb. He created you with a purpose, and intentionally for a purpose. He intricately planned who you would be with all the detail from your skin color, freckles, gray hairs, bald spots, and attitude, down to your personality and the crust you may or may not have on your feet. He blessed you with abilities, talents, and gifts that are to be used for His glory. God took one look at you and said, "Perfect."

No matter how you may look or feel right now, no matter whose approval you did or didn't get, no matter your accomplishments or failures, God loves, approves, and confirms all of you today. There's nothing you can do now or ever to change His blessings in your life. You may think, "If people knew my past or the things I have done, they would understand God cannot use me." Understand that when God sees you, He looks at you through His eyes, He separates you from your thoughts, past, and behavior. True HE may not be the biggest fan of some of your decisions and actions, but He wants to help you grow, become wiser, build a sense of discernment, and make better decisions.

Receive God's love and acceptance and allow Him to work in and through your life. Allow His love to empower, strengthen, and motivate you because you are blessed and equipped to live and walk in victory!

Accept His Timing

"Let us not become weary in doing good, for at the proper time we will reap a harvest if we do not give up." (Galatians 6:9, NIV)

How awesome would it be if we asked in faith and God answered immediately or at least within what we would consider a timely manner? We know that God's time does not always line up with our time. The Word tells us God is not like the man, He cannot lie, which means He is true to His word. He tells us if we are patient we will get to see His Word become a reality. If God just told us when we would get the spouse we wanted, or when we would get what we asked for, we would not have the faith and trust that He would do it, because it's already done. It takes faith to say "I don't know how, but I know He's going to do it. I don't know when, but I know He's going to fix it." It takes faith to say "I trust that my God said it and that completes it."

Ask daily "God, give me the grace and patience to accept Your timing." This means you are asking for God's strength, His supernatural empowerment to stand strong while you are waiting. Choose to keep believing, to praise Him, and to accept His timing knowing that He is faithful and has an abundance of blessings in store for your future!

The Best Time

"For the revelation awaits an appointed time; it speaks of the end and will not prove false. Though it lingers, wait for it; it will certainly come and will not delay." (Habakkuk 2:3, NIV)

The Word says, "The revelation awaits an appointed time." There specifically is a time determined for the fulfillment of the desires God has placed in your heart. God's appointed time is the best time; it's not too early that we are not ready, but not too late when we are not able to complete it! Even when we do not see the result we have to trust that God does and is pushing us towards it. He knows all the tools we will need to be a success. He knows the people who will teach us the lessons, build us up, help us, and He even knows our doubters and naysayers. If God gave us exactly what we asked for, we could be limiting what His blessings are by shooting too small when He wants to give us bigger.

This also plays into the people in your life. Like when babies are born, we give them baby food, but as they grow baby food will not sustain them and their growing bodies. Some people in our lives are good for the now, but where God is taking us, they may not be able to go. God sees and knows all; we have to trust in His timing. Just as we trust our physicians know what they are doing, trust that God knows what He's doing. Trust that at the right time, at the right place, He will release His promises in your life!

This is YOUR Season

"For the LORD God is a sun and shield; the LORD bestows favor and honor; no good thing does he withhold from those whose walk is blameless."
(Psalm 84:11, NIV)

This is the time and the season for God's people to experience a change. For those who have been faithful, have honored, and obeyed God's Word, I declare that He is about to put you in position to receive a favor that you didn't know you could receive or that you thought you were not worthy enough to receive. He is bestowing HIS favor, honor, and glory on you in a whole new way!

Decree doors are going to open for you that have not opened, or that you thought or spoke were closed. What should take you 40 years to accomplish, God is going to do in the twinkling of an eye. This is your season! All of a sudden, that dream will come to fruition. A promise will finally be fulfilled. Negative situations that have been plaguing you and holding you captive are going to turn around and work for your good. Get ready to receive, to rejoice, to grow, to prosper, and to achieve your dreams. This is YOUR season!

Declare your Shift is coming!

"You will also declare a thing, and it will be established for you; so the light will shine on your ways." (Job 22:28, NKJV)

Declare that a shift is coming right now in your life. Whatever you are standing in need of— a shift in your health, your finances, on the job, or even a shift in a relationship, its coming. What may look placid in the natural, is a raging storm in God's supernatural. A fresh wind from on high is about to push you and guide you in the right way! The enemies, troubles, pains, hardship you have seen in the past, you will see no more. Those addictions or bad habits that have held you captive in chains are being broken by the blood of Jesus. God's favor is being poured out on you in a way that will push you toward your destiny.

God is Jehovah Jireh, Lord, our Provider, not only will He provide, but His Word said HE would do exceedingly, abundantly above and beyond what we could ask or think. Have the attitude of God; I'm ready. I'm taking the limits off of You. I'm enlarging my vision. I may not see the plan, but I know You have the plan. Declare I'm coming into my shift!"

No Limit to His Power

"Surely the arm of the Lord is not too short to save, nor his ear too dull to hear." Isaiah 59:1 (NIV)

While the Israelites were in the desert headed for the Promised Land, God made sure to provide daily for them. In a desert where there is little to no life, they had manna to eat every day. As time passed, they begin to complain to Moses about what they did not have; they were unease by the lack of meat. Moses went to God, and God tells Moses He would provide meat for them. But God said whereas they are asking for a meal or one day, I will show my might and bless them with meat for the month.

Moses replied to God, "That's impossible. There are over two million people out here. If we butchered all of our flocks and herds, we still wouldn't have that much meat." God gave back the answer of all answers. He said, "Moses, is there any limit to My power?" He was telling Moses just because your eyes can not see a way, does not mean there is no way. When we bake a cake, we do not readily see the result but following the plan, we get the result. God is all-powerful and nothing is too hard for Him or beyond His control. Numbers 11:31, "God shifted the wind and brought quail in from the sea and caused them to fall into their camp."

Notice they didn't even have to go out and hunt or fish, scripture tells us the quail came to them. They didn't have to work for it they just had picked up and received the blessing. What am I trying to convey to you? God knows how to arrange things so that the blessings come to you. Trust in Him with all your might and lean not on your own understanding. Even in a dry and barren land, He will provide. There is no limit to God's power. So get ready to see those open doors of blessing in your life!

You Are a Masterpiece

"For we are God's masterpiece. He has created us a new in Christ Jesus, so we can do the good things he planned for us long ago." (Ephesians 2:10 NIV)

You are a masterpiece created by God Himself! That means you are not ordinary, average, normal, or a duplicate; you are a genuine one of a kind original. When God created you, He went to great lengths to make you exactly the way He wanted you. He gave you the right personality, gifts, talents, character, and pzazz. He enabled you to connect to the right connections to do exactly what He's called only you to do. The million dollar question is, do you walk, breathe, live, and act as the masterpiece you are or are you living as a cheap photocopy?

Don't settle for living just a standard mediocre life. Unlock the hidden treasures that God placed inside of you. Every morning remind yourself I am an original, authentic priceless masterpiece. I am handpicked and crafted by God; I am a person of extreme value and significance. You are an original—you were not created to be like everyone else; God designed you the way you are for a specific reason and purpose. Be who you are and walk in your authentic truths! You are fearfully and wonderfully made. Receive His love today because you are His most prized treasure!

Anointed to Be You

"I praise you because I am fearfully and wonderfully made; your works are wonderful, I know that full well." (Psalm 139:14, NIV)

Did you know that when you compare yourself to others or wish you were like someone else, it's like telling God you don't feel He made a mistake in creating you? It's almost as you see it as God made you inferior or less than He made everyone else. God did not make mistakes and didn't make anyone inferior. You are created exactly how He wants you to be, equipped with gifts and talents that are keen to only you. You are fully and totally equip for the race that's destined for you!

Keep the attitude that I may not have what they have, or be where they are, but I have what I need to be anointed to be me and do what God has for me to do. Don't try to be someone else, for you do not know their story and the things that they went through. You do know your story and the things you have been through and how you may have been through the fire, but you don't smell like smoke. Accept who you were created to be and walk in YOUR authority and not that of someone else.

Put Your Love into Action

"Suppose a believer who is rich enough to have all the necessities of life sees a fellow believer who is poor and does not have even basic needs. What if the rich believer does not help the poor one? Then it is clear that God's love is not in that person's heart. My children, our love should not be only words and talk. No, our love must be real. We must show our love for the things we do."
(1 John 3:17-18 ERV)

It has often been said that you can give without love, but you cannot love without giving. In this passage of scripture we are told love isn't just about our words and thoughts, it's about our actions. Love is about reaching out and meeting the needs of our fellow brothers and sisters. Sometimes loving someone is as simple as a smile, a hug, a compliment, or sharing a word of encouragement. You are the representation of God's love on Earth, how will you show love? We are blessed so that we can be a blessing to others. He wants to work through you to show His love and compassion to those we encounter.

Look for ways to put your love into action today and every day. The Word tells us that it's His kindness that leads people to repentance. He wants to show His kindness to the world through you. Step out and sow good seeds of love. God promises that those seeds will produce an abundant harvest in your life in return!

Praise like David Praised

"I praise you because I am fearfully and wonderfully made; your works are wonderful, I know that full well." (Psalm 139:14, NIV)

In this scripture, David is telling us that he is made perfectly by the will of God. He is gifted, talented, one of a kind, and fully equipped with what he needed. With this scripture, he said God had given me everything that I need for my journey in life. He praised God for making him in such an amazing way and declared that what God had done was wonderful. Is that how you see yourself?

People think they show humility by putting themselves down or downplaying their blessings. Things like it were no big deal, or it's nothing makes it seem like your blessings are trivial or have no value. We have to be bold and own our blessings like David.

Decide to stop putting yourself down; stop focusing on your flaws and comparing yourself to others. The Alpha and Omega says "you are a masterpiece." It's time to get in agreement with God and realize how much He loves you. It's time to realize how special you really are and how God loves you more than anything. Make the shift by changing your words and affirm yourself!

Your Alpha and Omega

"You could see my body grow each passing day. You listed all my parts, and not one of them was missing." (Psalms 139:16 ERV)

When God created you, He also planned out your days know the details of every second, minute, and hour. He knows every disappointment, loss, hurdle, trial, and tribulation; but the good news is that through Christ, your story always ends victoriously! God has a plan to bless and prosper you abundantly. When you follow Him and His plan, your results concludes with you fulfilling the destiny He has for you. When you go through the storms and the trials and tribulations of life, you have to turn the page and forge forward. You have to make the contentious decision to keep going and not given up. There is victory after this, but you can't give up the fight.

At times, we get so focused on what didn't work out that we stay stuck, relieving the disappointment over and over again. Recognize you have been like a hamster on an exercise wheel running in circles. It's time to let it go and turn the page to the new chapter God has in store. You may not have an understanding of it, it may not have even been fair, but remember, the next chapter is full of blessing, favor, and victory! Let go of the old and the past and move on towards your victorious future.

Welcome to the WTL

"how can we know the way?' Jesus answered, 'I am the way, the truth and the life. No one comes to the Father except through me."
(John 14:5–6, NIV)

Do you feel lost and disoriented, like you have no direction? Have you felt that your spiritual GPS has been disabled? Jesus said, "I am the way, the truth, and the life." Not only is He the Way to live in eternity, but Jesus is the way maker here on earth. He is the way to everything you need on this journey called life. You can apply Him to every situation in your life from finances, to the relationship, to work, to accomplish your dreams. When you know Jesus, you know the Way!

No matter what you may be going through or what opposition you may be facing, trust that He will make a way out of no way. Even when you don't see it, just trust that He is always working it out for you. Trust that He loves you more than anything that He wants to strengthen and endow you to live in complete total victory. Open your heart and your mind to the Way, Truth, and the Life to live in your victory.

I Know Who Holds Tomorrow

"The Lord shows us how we should live, and he is pleased when he sees people living that way." (Psalm 37:23, ERV)

People who aren't fulfilling their destiny will try to discourage you from fulfilling and achieving yours. It may not be intentional, but they constantly tell you what you can't. Family members, co-workers, and even your closest friends, try to talk you out of your dream, that's because God didn't put that promise and gift inside of them; He put it inside of you! If you keep believing, God will not only bring it to pass; He will do more than you can ask or think. Your future is in the hands of God, not man, so trust in God and not man.

Don't allow someone's disbelief to keep you from believing. Never let anyone talk you out of your dreams, goals, and aspirations. You are more than able to complete every assignment and overcome any and every obstacle. God said you are anointed, called, and appointed to fulfill every dream, goal, aspiration, and desire He's placed within you!

Hit the Delete Button

"So don't remember what happened in earlier times. Don't think about what happened a long time ago," (Isaiah 43:18, NIV)

Think of your mind like a computer, the way you program it will determine how it will function. If you had the most expensive, powerful, sophisticated, advanced computer in the world, but if loaded with the wrong software, it's not going to perform at its best. In the same manner, many people are not living a victorious life, not because there is something wrong with them, but because of what they have set their minds on. They start believing the lies; I have no talents, I am not smart enough, I'm not good enough, in my past I can't... Just like a virus can slow down a perfectly good computer, wrong thinking can keep us from our destiny. Change your thought process to change your outlook.

Reprogram Your Mind

"Don't change yourselves to be like the people of this world, but let God change you inside with a new way of thinking. Then you will be able to understand and accept what God wants for you. You will be able to know what is good and pleasing to him and what is perfect." (Romans 12:2 NIV)

People don't realize that the reason they're not happy, not enjoying life is simply that think in the wrong direction. They've programmed their minds to worry and stress. They've programmed their minds to complain and focus on the negative. Just as we train our mind to focus on the negative, we can also reprogram our minds to focus on the positive. Focusing on the Word of God and His promises reprograms our mind to think positively. Meditating on God's goodness develops a right mindset of seeing the good in the bad. Choosing to be grateful and focus on what's right rather than what's wrong, we are choosing to have a positive attitude and outlook. This is not automatic; you have to discipline yourself to focus on the right things. You have to make a conscious effort to spend time in the Word of God every single day until a habit is formed.

Choose Your Friends Wisely

"Don't be fooled: "Bad friends will ruin good habits."
(1 Corinthians 15:33 ERV)

To embrace the full destiny God has destined for you, you must be willing to make changes in your life. You have to be willing to examine where you are and what you need and may need to do to move forward. This may include separating yourself from some friends that you spend a lot of time with. Remember people are like trees, some are your roots, some the trunk, branches, and some leaves. In this new season, for you to rise higher, you have to break away from ships that are limiting you (friendships, relationships, partnerships, etc). You have to develop new relationships with people who are going to pull you up and inspire you to rise higher.

This also includes separating yourself from people who are holding you back spiritually. My pastor often says if you are the smartest person in your circle, you need a new circle. Find people who will challenge you and push you to the next level to become everything God's created you to be. Remember, he who walks with the wise become wise. Choose your friends wisely and don't be deceived, surround yourself with people who willl cause you to rise higher so you can live in the destiny God has in store for you!

Breaking Strongholds

"and they all drank the same spiritual drink. They drank from that spiritual rock that was with them, and that rock was Christ."
(1 Corinthians 10:4 ERV)

The Words says that there is a battle going on in our minds. Your thoughts tend to dictate your actions. That's why the adversary will do everything he can to get you thinking negative about everything in life. It's not our thoughts that are holding us back; sometimes it's that we've believed the negative things that other people have spoken over our dreams, aspirations, goals, and life. Words are like seeds, if you dwell on them, giving them "water and nutrients," long enough, they'll take root and become your truths.

In life, there will always be people telling you what cannot be done, and speaking negative things. It's easy for us to latch on to negative words and develop what the scripture calls a "stronghold." That's a wrong thought or action that keeps us from receiving God's best. The way you break those negative strongholds is by rejecting the lie, forgiving the person, and embracing the truth of God's Word.
Destroy the negative strongholds and embrace God's truth so you can be all that God has called you to be!

The Same Favor

"Jesus Christ is the same yesterday, today, and forever."
(Hebrews 13:8, NIV)

One of the most important reasons to know God and study His Word is that you learn His promises and come to understand the character of God. The way He has blessed others, He will also bless you. The same favor that was poured out over many throughout the history of the Bible and history in general will be shown to you. The blessings that were poured out on Abraham, Elijah and Joseph God wants to give and pour out on you. He wants to open doors, line up supernatural appointments, and bring new increase and provision to your life. The question is, are you ready and willing to receive it? Can you see it with your eyes of faith?

You've heard it said countless times God is the same yesterday, today and forever. He is always with you and forever for you. Even before you see things turn around, believe that He is working on your behalf to turn it around. When He pours out His favor, it won't be just a drizzle; it's going to be a great flood — a flood of ideas, good breaks, of talent, of grace, of favor. Keep believing, keep hoping and keep praising because the same favor that was back then is the same favor now, and more importantly is coming your way!

Exceptional Favor

"The path of the righteous is like the morning sun, shining ever brighter till the full light of day." (Proverbs 4:18 NIV)

We all face challenges every second, minute, hour, day, week, month, and year of our lives. We all have trials and tribulations to overcome. If we keep the right perspective, it will help us maintain faith so that we can move forward into prosperity. In the present moment, life may seem to be overwhelming or overpowering, but these challenges are for those who are natural beings having a spiritual experience. You are not natural. God breathed His life into you making you a supernatural being having a natural experience. You are exceptional, and exceptional people face exceptional difficulties in life.

However, we serve an exceptional God! He'll pour out His exceptional grace, exceptional wisdom and exceptional favor to get us through whatever we face! When life gives you an extraordinary problem; instead of being discouraged, be encouraged knowing that you're an extraordinary person with an extraordinary future. Stand firm in faith, declaring victory for your future, keep declaring all of God's promises. Keep declaring that you are moving forward into the exceptional life the Lord has in store for you!

Press toward the Promise

"...imitators of those who through faith and patience inherit the promises."
(Hebrews 6:12, ERV)

Do you feel discouraged about something you've been asking God for a while now? Remember through faith and patience; you will see God's promises come to fruition. Understand that the enemy always fights the hardest when he knows you are at your breakthrough. He would not bother you if he thought you were going just to settle and stay in mediocrity. Run on toward the promise given to you by God, through faith and patience; you will get there. Don't be like the Israelites and talk yourself out of your promise. No, don't look at the size of the obstacles in your life, but look at the size of God in your life. Lift up your eyes to the hills from which come your help, knowing you serve Almighty God. Be like Abraham who believed God even when his circumstances looked and seemed impossible. God rewards the people who seek Him, stand firm in faith, and keep believing. As you press toward your promised destiny, you will see God's hand of favor, grace, mercy, and blessing.

fore Your Eyes

"who forgives all your sins and heals all your diseases," (Psalm 103:3 NIV)

In this passages of the Psalm, David was ascertained to honor the Lord with his mind. David knew that what he watched would affect his thinking. If he didn't protect and cover his mind by monitoring what he observed, he would be tempted to do things that would not please the Lord.
This rule remains true even in modern times. What we subject our body and minds to will affect our spirit. Surrounding yourself with negative things will lead you to have a negative mindset and vibe. When we give power and authority to things that are not of God's will and destiny for us, we allow strongholds to begin to grow. God has given us the power and authority to destroy those strongholds through Jesus Christ!

If you are battling thoughts that are holding you back or keeping you in bondage, you can break free! Begin to know that God forgives you and does not hold your past against you. Things they said you did, things you actually did, and even the things you thought about doing. God said for His own sake He does not remember, so you have to let them go and receive His forgiveness. Then look at the lesson you learned from the situation and grow from it, let it propel your closer to your destiny not away from it. Honor God for all that He has done, is doing, will do, and even for the things He may not have done or will do, this is when you are walking by faith, and you can live your life through His eyes before your eyes.

This Battle is Not Yours its the Lords

"The Lord will fight for you; you need only to be still." (Exodus 14:14 NIV)

No matter how successful you become in life, you will always have people who criticize you. No matter how good your news is, someone will try to find the darkness in your joy. One thing we should always remember is you don't have to respond to everything. Sometimes silent speak more than words. We were told when someone goes low; you go high. Your high is when you go to your father in Heaven who will fight all your battles on your behalf. You have to just receive and walk in the victory.

My mother would tell me that you cannot please everyone and everyone will not like you. When your enemies come against you, it is easy for us to get defensive and want to clap back. Just as Jesus told His disciples, you have to speak peace over their homes. Speak peace over their homes, their minds, and their lives. If they do not receive that peace, the Bible tells us it will come back to you. This means if they are not willing to be at peace with you, that peace will come back and you will be at peace with them.

When you give them peace, it puts you at peace, and if they reject it just like that, you got double for your trouble. Remember a saying a coach once told me" When people are acting a monkey, it is not your circus, not your monkey." Be at peace with things and people knowing that this battle is not yours to fight anyway, it's the Lords.

The Strength of Praise

"The LORD is my strength and my shield; my heart trusts in him, and I am helped. My heart leaps for joy, and I will give thanks to him in song." (Psalm 28:7, NIV)

In the spiritual realm of life when you praise God, you will find you get the remarkable strength to endure life challenges. We have to praise him even when we do not see the answers, and that is what will keep you encourage when doubt wants to take over.

Complaining and constant bickering gets you nowhere and accomplishes nothing, the most it will do is drain you of all your energy and strength to overcome the obstacle. You can't remain positive if all you focus on is the negative. The bank account may look slim, but you know your God is a provider. People may talk and bash your name and character, but you know your God to be all powerful. When you praise you leap, when you wallow you just jump. Leaping no matter how big or small takes you forward. Jumping no matter how high puts you back in the same place.

Leap in advance and thank God in advance for what He is going to do and is completing in your life. It's easy to be grateful in hindsight, but true worship and praise is done in advance. Doing so also prepares you to receive what He will give to you. You will be able to boldly embrace your destiny with strength. Remember to praise Him in advance and receive His strength to endure.

While Waiting

"Be patient, then, brothers and sisters, until the Lord's coming. See how the farmer waits for the land to yield its valuable crop, patiently waiting for the autumn and spring rains." (James 5:7 NIV)

God has placed dreams and desires inside of us. These dreams and desires are like crops grown by a farmer; it takes times for the crops to grow and mature. The same is with our dreams and desires we have to wait until the appointed time for us to reap them. It could be waiting for marriage, promotion, business to manifest, a relationship, or even waiting to heal from sickness or addiction. We have to trust and believe that God knows the right time to flood us with His blessings. Too quickly we get discouraged, anxious, or even fearful when things don't happen in our time, we have to remember God's time is not always our time, but His time is always right on time! No matter what you are praying, expecting, or hoping for, see things to changing in your favor before you see them changing. Today could be the day.

Where Strength and Joy are Found

"Splendor and majesty are before him; strength and joy are in his dwelling place." (1 Chronicles 16:27 NIV)

How would you like more joy in your life? The joy that fills to overflowing. Or how about more strength to endure this roller coaster ride we call life? God tells us that in His presence there is the fullness of joy. This is that complete joy that the world didn't give and the world cannot take away. When you have His joy, He throws in at no additional charge His strength which is not like our strength. God's strength is a supernatural strength that enables us to withstand and defeat any attack of the enemy. When God is for you, then who or what could stand against you? Absolutely NOTHING!!!

This verse says that His strength and joy are in His dwelling place, His dwelling place is in His tabernacle. God's tabernacle is not a building that we can go to because we are His tabernacle. He promises that He inhabits the praises of His people. He dwells on the inside of us giving us His strength and His joy; we just have to tap into it.

Anytime you feel down and out, defeated or overwhelmed, just go into a fit of praise declaring God' goodness and faithfulness. In doing so, He will fill you with His joy and strength all the days of your life!

A Flood is Coming

"If he holds back the rain, the earth will dry up. If he lets the rain lose, it will flood the land." (Job 12:15 ERV)

Has it ever rained so hard that the weatherperson announces that a particular area is under a Flash Flood Warning? What that means is enough water and fallen that could produce the right circumstances for a flood. In our lives, God has issued a Flash Flood Warning! He has spoken and said the conditions are favorable for the windows of heaven to open up and begin to pour you out such a blessing you will not have room enough to receive. God is flooding you with His grace, mercy, favor, goodness, healing, joy, protection, and countless other things. He is pouring out blessings that you did not think you even deserved. When God makes it rain, it pours! In the famous words from the Color Purple, "It's gonna rain on your head!" Receive God rain today.

Open the Floodgates

"He guided them safely. They had nothing to fear. He drowned their enemies in the sea." Psalms 78:53 (NIV)

A tsunami nothing can stop the force of this rushing water. A few feet of water can move a thousand pound car like it was a piece of paper. You've seen the footage of the aftermath of various flood throughout the world and the devastation they have causes. Now you may ask how does the destruction of a flood motivate me to be all that God has called me to be? You may have obstacles that look insurmountable; dreams that look unattainable, goals that seem unreachable, be encouraged: when God releases the flood of His power, nothing can stop you.

That illness may look like it will win, but when the flood of healing starts raging, it doesn't stand a chance. Your opposition may be stronger, better financed, and better equipped; but when God opens the floodgates, remember He does choose the equipped, He equips the chosen. When God equips you nothing can stop you.

You say well I am not connected to the right people to make my dreams work when God opened the floodgates people will come to you from all directions aligning with what God spoke. Do prepare yourself for a sprinkle of God's mercy, a stream of His grace, a river of His favor, now get ready for a tsunami of His increase and it is coming your way!

Any Moment

"Then the Lord said, "I am making this agreement with all of your people. I will do amazing things that have never before been done for any other nation on earth. The people with you will see that I, the Lord, am very great. They will see the wonderful things that I will do for you." (Exodus 34:10 ERV)

God said, "I'm going to do amazing things that I have never done for any other nation on earth. People will see what great things I can do because I'm going to do something awesome for you." I love how God is very specific with His words; He did not say I will do good or nice things, He said I would do amazing things. It may not look like it right now; but remember, we have trust that He has a plan. We have to see the end throughout the process. At any moment, you could meet the right person that will have what you need to achieve that goal. At any moment, God could do something amazing that you have never seen or expected in your life.

Now the real question is, will you be patient and wait for God's moment? Every voice will tell you why this is not for you or will not happen for you, but God wants to do something amazing in your life! Why don't you get into agreement with Him, instead of listening to what you cannot do, listen to the voice that says you may just succeed, you will accomplish that goal. Tell yourself what God has for me it is for me and can't no devil in hell stop my God. Shaking off doubt, negativity, disappointment, self-pity, small dreams and goals and set your sights on the stars, it could happen at any moment.

Hold on Help is on the Way

"The king of Assyria only has men. But we have the Lord our God with us! Our God will help us. He will fight our battles!" So King Hezekiah of Judah encouraged the people and made them feel stronger."
(2 Chronicles 32:8 ERV)

When we are born, we are told our lives will be filled with trial and tribulations. As a child, we begin by battling small things like minor illnesses, scrapes, and bruises. As we get older those attacks intensify and become a lot bigger ranging from job loss, disabilities, emotional distress, and more which are all attacks of the enemy. As an adult, we have to remember when the enemy attacks we do not fight back alone. We don't have to fight at all for we know God will fight our battles. So when the enemy attacks, God reacts. God doesn't wait and see what the outcome will be; He waits for us to turn it over to Him to work out He waits for us to yield to His will and abilities.

God is close to those with a broken heart. God knows you got a bad prognosis or diagnosis. He knows when you are struggling financially. He knows when you have been used, abused, and mistreated. You may not see anything happening, but you can be assured that God is not only aware, but He is handling it. He already has mapped out the solution. If you keep the faith and don't give up, at the right time, He will release His power of healing and restoration. He not only brought you to it, but He will bring you through it, and He will bring you out, but the good news is He will bring you out better off than you were before!

Resurrection Power

"...He is risen from the dead, just as he said would happen..."
(Matthew 28:6, NIV)

Every Easter the whole Christian community celebrates the power of the Resurrection of Jesus Christ. We celebrate the fact that on the third day He got up with all power in His hands. Did you know that every day you have a reason to celebrate because He got up? The God we serve is alive and His "Get Up" power didn't end with the cross, He is just as active today as he was back then. The same power that resurrected Jesus resurrects life into all areas of your life.

Whether your dream is to be debt free, a homeowner, or free from the burden of poverty, resurrection power can be applied. You are never limited when you have the authority and power of Christ to back you. Stop selling yourself short, aim higher, ask questions, make the moves, get your hopes up, and get your expectations up! God is faithful to His Word and will have His resurrection power flowing in every area of your life.

It is Completed

"being confident of this, that he who began a good work in you will carry it on to completion until the day of Christ Jesus." (Philippians 1:6 NIV)

In movies often what we think means something ends up meaning something completely different.

When Jesus was on the cross, His final words were "It is finished." To many, it would be assumed He was referring to His work and His life as being finished. In actuality, He was saying, Father, I have completed my assignments assigned to me now I have trust and confidence that you will not finish what you have started. What people assumed was the ending was the beginning.

When things look dismal in life like things will not go the way you desire for them to go, make the declaration in your life that it is finished. This declaration says, God, I am trusting that you are going to turn this situation around in my favor. When you turn it over to God you are saying I know my healing is on the way, I know my family will be restored, I know my finances will improve. Always speak victory over your situations regardless of what the outcome looks like it may be. God is faithful and will bring to completion that which He has started in you.

72 Hours

"They will flog Him and kill Him, and on the third day He will rise again." (Luke 18:33, NIV)

One of my favorite shows is the first 48. It talks about various police cases and how they have to get a good lead in the first 48 hours before the case starts to go cold. If Jesus final moments had a show, it would be "The Last First 72." His last hours are seen as the most gruesome, painful, discouraging, and even defeating the thought that it was over. It seemed like the adversary won and God lost. Remember, when God has a plan for your life not even death and stop it. 72 hours later a big break came in the case. The body that they thought was dead was missing. It was found to be walking among the living, a walking living breathing miracle.

Regardless of what it seems, regardless of the amount of time you have had to endure, regardless of the number of people telling you-you will fail, it won't work, give up; if you keep the faith, stand strong in God, and He will make you a living breathing miracle. He will show your naysayers and doubters that He holds all power and authority in his hands. God always completes what He begins!

he Un-

"For those who find me find life and receive favor from the Lord."
(Proverbs 8:35 NIV)

Have you ever wanted someone to love you for you, your good, bad, ugly, and indifferent? Someone who would be there for you no matter what you say or do? Well, the good news is God loves you unconditionally. He loves your good and bad. He even loves the smelly socks when you get home from a long day. Not only does He love you HE is also for you. This means He has your best interest in mind and heart.

This is called God's favor! Sometimes in your life, even if you haven't or didn't recognize it, you have all experienced God's favor. It is simply His UN-deserved, UN-earned, UN-explainable goodness in your life. This favor brings about blessings that you did not ask for or did not do anything to warrant. His favor protects, promotes, and opens doors for you. God's favor takes you places that you could never go on your own.

Declare over your life that shortly, the very near future, God is going to unleash His unprecedented favor in your life — favor as you've never seen before! The key is to stay connected to Him, through prayer, worship, praise, and reading His Word. Let Him guide your step and your thoughts. As you pour yourself out to Him, He will pour out Himself on you! His grace, mercy and supernatural, UN-deserved, UN-earned, UN-explainable favor in every area of your life!

Unparalleled Power

"And you will know that God's power is very great for us who believe. It is the same as the mighty power" (Ephesians 1:19 ERV)

We all have heard the saying God has been so good to me. We have all witnessed at some point in our lives God's grace, or seen Him protect us, promote us, or open doors for us. This is not by happenstance; this is God's favor in your life. But as true as the world turns God is about to pour out an unparalleled amount of favor like never before seen.

The Word said that God's power is not just great, but it is VERY great for those who believe. When you think about our lives everything, we need run off of power. From our computers, phones, televisions, cars, everything has a power source. How great is it to know that we are connected to the greatest power sources there is.

The word "unparalleled" means "unmatched, unprecedented, for the first time." Meaning what God has done before in your life He will not do the same way again, He will do it greater. Your destiny is bigger, better, and greater; it is unparalleled to anything you can imagine. You have to stay tapped into the source to obtain the resources. Your power bill has been paid and your power is flowing. Let your light shine and nothing dim it.

Make it a Great Day

"So I say to you: Ask, and it will be given to you; seek, and you will find; knock and the door will be opened to you" (Luke 11:9, NIV)

When you leave a person presence a common farewell is "Have a great day." When you say have a great day you are giving an opportunity for it not to be a great day. Are you looking for God's favor? Do you anticipate His blessings falling on you? So many people wake up daily and just want to make it through the day. What God has planned for you and your future is way more than a good day. If you stand true to your faith, walking by faith and not by sight, you will see things you never even dreamed come to pass.

No matter where you are in life, no matter what's happening around you, start seeking more of God's favor. Don't settle for normal or mediocrity. Don't settle for living paycheck to paycheck Believe that God is great, and He wants to and will do more in and through you. The Word tells us, what we seek, we will find. Seek Him first, and He will pour out His supernatural favor upon you!

Let the Encouragement Flow

"Worry weighs a person down; an encouraging word cheers a person up" (Proverbs 12:25, NIV)

How do you respond when you see someone who is discouraged or struggling? Remember life and death are in the power of your tongue, what you say could keep them going or put a little pep in their step. With the condition of the world, we have to motivate and encourage one another more than ever. Tell people how much you love them now, tell them you value them. Uplift creativity and talented let them know the sky is just the base; the stars are the limit. Always remember, your words have power and authority and carry the very essence of life in them. You carry hope, healing, encouragement, and fresh starts, and you can pour it out everywhere you go.

Choose to speak positive and give encouragement to anyone who crosses your path. Choose to speak victory and faith over failure and defeat. Instead of telling people what they are not doing right and pointing out their faults, find what they are doing right and build on their strengths. There are already more than enough critical and judgmental people in the world. Choose to be the person who lifts up others and restore them.

Get Excited About Your Future!

"But the path of the righteous is like the light of dawn, which shines brighter and brighter until full day" (Proverbs 4:18, ERV)

You may have a lot going on and feel like things are all over the place, but if you are walking in the authority of Jesus Christ, you know you have reasons beyond imagination to be excited about your future. Even if things seem dark and dismal right now, weeping may endure for the night, but joy comes in the morning light. You have to remember that God does not do things by happenstance; He does everything for a reason and a purpose. You have the destiny to fulfill and no matter what it seems like He is not through with you yet. Your best has not come to pass, just yet.

God is the God of increase. Your past was just the lesson to prepare you for your blessing. God wants to bring out strength and talents in you that you did not even think you had. He wants you to win, but also everything attached to you will win. Keep pushing forward, keep fighting, and keep believing because God is preparing an overflow with your name on it.

eeds of Greatness

"His divine power has given us all things that pertain to life and godliness, through the knowledge of Him who called us by glory and virtue."
(2 Peter 1:3, NKJV)

When God stopped what He was doing to create you, He created perfection. Therefore, He equipped you with everything you need to fulfill the calling on your life. He gave you the passion and ability to complete and conquer all task assigned to you. No dream is too big, no challenge too hard, with God on your side the sky is the foundation, the stars are your limit.

A lot of times we overlook our potential because what we pose seems subtle to us. It may not seem like it is a big deal when we first realize it, but it begins as a seed. A mighty redwood begins as a mere seed. With proper tending to it begins to grow and develop into a tree over 375 feet tall. Imagine how the seed God has planted in you can grow and not only how big it can become, but how life-changing it could be for you and those around you.

How do you tend to and nurture your seed? I'm glad you asked, by meditating on, studying, and reading the Word of God. Keeping Him first in all that we do, will keep clear direction for your life. He promises to lead you and guide you as you draw closer to him. He is the ultimate gardener, and He produces a bountiful harvest.

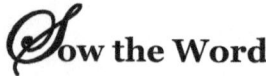ow the Word

"The sower sows the word." (Mark 4:14, ERV)

Every spring farmers go to the fields and begin planting seeds for their fall harvest. The Word of God is like a seed; when it is planted inside of you, it will come to produce not just a harvest, but a bountiful harvest. So how can you begin to plant the seeds of God's Word in your life? Begin by putting work to it. By applying His Word to every aspect of your life and following His commandments, the seed will begin to grow.

Just as the farmer plants in good soil you have to make sure the soil you are planting God's Word in is good soil. You can't plant success in soil that is filled with defeat and doubt. You can't plant healing in soil that is filled with I will never be healed. You can plant deliverance in soil that is plagued with the addiction. Prosperity can grow where there is jealousy and constant comparison. Have a forgiving mind and a humble heart to sow your seeds upon. As you remain steadfast in the Word and have unmovable faith, you will see all His plans for you start to come to fruition and produce a bountiful harvest in your life.

What Can God Do Through You?

"The Lord is with you, you mighty man of valor!" (Judges 6:12, ERV)

People think that because God is all great and powerful, He doesn't care about us individually, or feel anything they do for Him is inadequate. God sees us as His children, just as when a child gives you a gift you smile and value it because of its sentimental value. God sees you as perfect and holds every praise, every worship, every hallelujah, and every thank you, Jesus, to His heart. In His eyes, you lack nothing in Him!

In this periscope of text Gideon was hiding out from his enemies, he was afraid and didn't feel equipped to do what God called him to do. Gideon was focused on his circumstances and his limitations, but God was more focus on what He could do through Gideon. Gideon felt weak, but God saw him as strong. Gideon felt unqualified, but God saw him as ready to do the job. Gideon felt insecure, but God saw him as full of boldness. When Gideon obeyed God, even against all the odds, he ended in victory!

Do you have Gideon experiences? Are you focused on your limitations and circumstances? Do you feel weak, unqualified, unequipped, insecure, and doubtful of your ability to achieve, succeed, or achieve? Look in the mirror at yourself and speak over yourself that you are more than able to do anything you set your mind and heart to through Christ. With God, it is not about how you feel, how others feel about you, how others view you or even how you see yourself. It is about what God has spoken to you and how He sees you through His eyes. You have to yield your own natural to God's supernatural. When you trust and obey God beyond your circumstances, that's when His powers activate, and mountains are moved. That is when He can work with you and bring abundance in every area of your life.

Get Excited About Your Future!

"But the path of the righteous is like the light of dawn, which shines brighter and brighter until full day" (Proverbs 4:18, ERV)

You may have a lot going on and feel like things are all over the place, but if you are walking in the authority of Jesus Christ, you know you have reasons beyond imagination to be excited about your future. Even if things seem dark and dismal right now, weeping may endure for the night, but joy comes in the morning light. You have to remember that God does not do things by happenstance, He does everything for a reason and a purpose. You have a destiny to fulfill, and no matter what it seems like He is not through with you yet. Your best has not come to pass, just yet.

God is the God of increase. Your past was just the lesson to prepare you for your blessing. God wants to bring out strength and talents in you that you did not even think you had. He wants you to win, but also everything attached to you will win. Keep pushing forward, keep fighting, and keep believing because God is preparing an overflow with your name on it.

Seeds of Greatness

"His divine power has given us all things that pertain to life and godliness, through the knowledge of Him who called us by glory and virtue." (2 Peter 1:3, NKJV)

When God stopped what He was doing to create you, He created perfection. Therefore, He equipped you with everything you need to fulfill the calling on your life. He gave you the passion and ability to complete and conquer all task assigned to you. No dream is too big, no challenge too hard, with God on your side the sky is the foundation, the stars are your limit.

A lot of times we overlook our potential because what we pose seems subtle to us. It may not seem like it is a big deal when we first realize it, but it begins as a seed. A mighty redwood begins as a mere seed. With proper tending to it begins to grow and develop into a tree over 375 feet tall. Imagine how the seed God has planted in you can grow and not only how big it can become, but how life-changing it could be for you and those around you.

How do you tend to and nurture your seed? I'm glad you asked, by meditating on, studying, and reading the Word of God. Keeping Him first in all that we do, will keep clear direction for your life. He promises to lead you and guide you as you draw closer to him. He is the ultimate gardener, and He produces a bountiful harvest.

Sow the Word

"The sower sows the word." (Mark 4:14, ERV)

Every spring farmers go to the fields and begin planting seeds for their fall harvest. The Word of God is like a seed; when it is planted inside of you, it will come to produce not just a harvest, but a bountiful harvest. So how can you begin to plant the seeds of God's Word in your life? By putting work to it. By applying His Word to every aspect of your life and following His commandments, the seed will begin to grow.

Just as the farmer plants in good soil you have to make sure the soil you are planting God's Word in is good soil. You can't plant success in soil that is filled with defeat and doubt. You can't plant healing in soil that is filled with I will never be healed. You can plant deliverance in soil that is plagued with the addiction. Prosperity can grow where there are jealousy and constant comparison. Have a forgiving mind and a humble heart to sow your seeds upon. As you remain steadfast in the Word and have unmovable faith, you will see all His plans for you start to come to fruition and produce a bountiful harvest in your life.

What Can God Do Through You?

"The Lord is with you, you mighty man of valor!" (Judges 6:12, ERV)

People think that because God is all great and powerful, He doesn't care about us individually, or feel anything they do for Him is inadequate. God sees us as His children, just as when a child gives you a gift you smile and value it for its sentimental value. God sees you as perfect and holds every praise, every worship, every hallelujah, and every thank you, Jesus, to His heart. In His eyes, you lack nothing in Him!

In this periscope of text Gideon was hiding out from his enemies, he was afraid and didn't feel equipped to do what God called him to do. Gideon was focused on his circumstances and his limitations, but God was focused on what He could do through Gideon. Gideon felt weak, but God saw him as strong. Gideon felt unqualified, but God saw him as ready to do the job. Gideon felt insecure, but God saw him as full of boldness. When Gideon obeyed God, even against all the odds, he ended in victory!

Do you have a Gideon experience? Are you more focused on your limitations and circumstances? Do you feel weak, unqualified, unequipped, insecure, and doubtful of your ability to achieve, succeed, or achieve? Look in the mirror at yourself and speak over yourself that you are more than able to do anything you set your mind and heart to through Christ. With God, it is not about how you feel, how others feel about you, how others view you or even how you see yourself. It is about what God has spoken to you and how He sees you through His eyes. You have to yield your own natural to Gods supernatural. When you trust and obey God beyond your circumstances, that's when His powers activate, and mountains are moved. That is when He can work with you and bring abundance in every area of your life.

Bigger

"because everyone who is a child of God has the power to win against the world." (1 John 5:4 ERV)

When you look in the side view mirrors of a car, the writing says objects appear closer than they really are. The same applies to things that we fear. A spider, the size of a penny, looks to be the size of a basketball. Things that are like ant mounds appear to be the size of Mount Everest, larger than they really are. The reason for this is that fear paralyzes your mind. It causes you to become worried, anxious, uptight, and easily be panicked. Fear causes us to lose sight and become unfocused on the Word and promises of God. You begin to doubt that God is present and working in your favor, you begin to question does He care. Remember fear only has the power and authority that you give it. Whatever the fear is to tell it I am not afraid for I am more than a conqueror. God has given you all power and authority in heaven and on earth, utilize that power. Anytime fear shows up repeat and declares no weapon formed against you shall prosper.

No matter the size of your fear, remember how big your God is. You've probably heard these saying before but if God is for you then who or what can stand against you. Greater is the God that is in you than he that is in the world. God is bigger than the universe, bigger than the sun and the stars. Therefore, He is bigger than all the things that come against you! Let your faith rise and be bigger!

Remember, no matter how big fear seems, it's no match for the power of your Almighty God. When you yield yourself to Him, you tap into His power. Greater is He that is in you than he that is in the world. God is bigger than your problems and bigger than fear. Let faith rise in your heart because faith is the victory that overcomes the world.

Clearing the Cloud called Fear

"By day the LORD went ahead of them in a pillar of cloud to guide them on their way and by night in a pillar of fire to give them light so that they could travel by day or night."
(Exodus 13:21, NIV)

Fear is extremely over exaggerated in our minds, which transcends into our reality. When a cloud is low to the ground, it is called for. Fear is like a cloud it sits up high and out of reach, but when we give it the power it lowers itself and began to block our vision. Its purpose is to keep you from seeing the light at the end of the tunnel, or to keep you from seeing your purpose in destiny.

How do you clear the cloud and see the clear blue sky God has in store for you. The Bible tells us the story of the Israelites who were led toward their Promised Land with a cloud by day and a cloud of fire by night; it was the cloud of God's glory. The cloud of His glory is where you'll find joy, strength, peace, love, and protection. It's where you find God's vision and direction. God inhabits the praise of His people, when you are faced with fear go into crazy praise and watch the fog raise. When you praise Him, He shows up and lifts the fog of fear so you can clearly see the good plan He has in store for you!

Bold as a Lion

"The wicked are afraid of everything, but those who live right are as brave as lions." (Proverbs 28:1 ERV)

We are called to live a life that is upfront, audacious, assured, and victorious. We go through storms that may cause us to bend, but we don't break. We don't have to live with the weight and pressure of fear and anxiety dwindling over us. When Jesus died on the cross, He took with Him our fear, worry, and uncertainty. When you rise in faith, knowing that God is with you and for you, all doubt and fear has to leave your life.

When you are righteous, the Word tells us to be bold as a lion. Righteousness is God's way of doing things in our lives. When we submit to His way, He gives us His power to be bold and have the strength to endure all the test and trials of life. When life begins to make you feel anxious, fearful, or doubtful, declare the Word of God over your life, and it will set you free!

Destroy Negative Labels

"I praise you because you made me in such a wonderful way. I know how amazing that was!" (Psalms 139:14 NIV)

People have called you names from birth. Some of those names are good names, and some of them are not. Some of them are true, and some of them are lies. I have always been told you may be called a lot of things, but you do not have to answer to everything you are called. When people call you names that are not who you are you do not have to take ownership of them. When people call you a failure, weak, incompetent, or say that you are in lack, do not claim those titles. Center yourself around people who speak life and faith into you.

Oprah Winfrey was told that she was too emotional and not right for television. She was intelligent enough not to take ownership of that label and went on to have a number one television show for 24 consecutive seasons. The common denominator of successful people is that they chose to remove the negative labels and find a silver lining in negative situations. It's in this same manner that we must operate as people of God. Disregard what other people speak of your life if it is not in alignment with the plan of God and what He has spoken over your life. Remove the negative label, negative thoughts, negative people, and negative vibe from your life and be who God created you to be.

imitless

"To all perfection, I see a limit, but your commands are boundless."
(Psalm 119:96 NIV)

The God we serve is all knowing and all powerful. He can do what we may not be able to see it able to do ourselves. When we make decisions that are not favorable or blatantly do wrong, He does not stop caring or using us. No matter what our past looks like, or what our ethnic background is, our family history, rumors, lies, truths, or any other factor man may hold against you God can and will still use you. He knew your destiny when He created you; this included your beginning, your mistakes, your successes, and your ending.

When people attempt to place you in bondage, you have the power and authority given to you to break those chains. All you have to do is have faith. Faith will help you do the impossible; faith will help you move the immovable, faith will help you overcome anything that stands in your way. Doors are not just opened they are blown off the hinges pouring our opportunity after opportunity. Remove negativity and watch you become the lender and not the borrower, the head and not the tail, above and not beneath. Take off bondage that is making you do the speed limit, with God and your faith you are limitless in the possibilities.

reat is His Mercy

"For the LORD is good; His mercy is everlasting, and His truth endures to all generations." (Psalm 100:5, NIV)

Have you ever messed up in life, or made a mistake that you felt bad about? You already felt bad about the situation, but then other people came in and added more fuel to the fire. They remind you of how you failed and how you shouldn't have even tried, or they use that one mistake to put down any attempt you may try to better yourself. You have to remind yourself that although you fell, you serve a God who will pick you back up again. People will often try to hold you down because they are held down. Everyone who says they want to see you succeed, don't really want to see you succeed. You have to ask yourself do I have people around me who are building me up to see how hard I fall, or are they building me up because they genuinely want to see me succeed and prosper. Surround yourself with eagles and you will soar, surround yourself with chickens and you will become a meal.

Keep in mind when God created you He created you in His image. This means you are not, and nothing about you is a mistake. His great mercy has equipped you with all you will need to survive this show called life. You have the right personality, characteristics, attitude, gifts, talents, look, smile, even the right completion for the journey. When you fail, because you will, it is just your First Attempt In Learning. Keep in your Future Always Involves Learning as well. Through His mercy learn from your mistake, dust yourself off, and try again and again and again. Embrace the victorious future God has in store for you!

Your Assignment

"We are therefore Christ's ambassadors, as though God were making his appeal through us. We implore you on Christ's behalf: Be reconciled to God." (2 Corinthians 5:20, NIV)

When God created you, He did so with a purpose, not happenstance. He said there are somethings and people that you are assigned to bless and touch that no one else can. What this means is that you have a job to do that no one else can do. You have a life to save that no doctor can save. You have a business to start that no other person can start. You have the destiny to fulfill that no one else can fulfill. God has chosen you to be you! As crazy, smart, temperamental as you may be, God wants you! You are the piece of His divine puzzle that no one else can fit. He wants your talents, gifts, smile, love, passion, and your tenacity. You are uniquely created for a specific purpose. Your uniqueness makes you a part of His royal kingdom; you are royalty. You may not fully understand or know your assignment, but hasten to His throne and allow Him to guide you. Keep your faith and your eyes stayed on Jesus, and your assignment will show itself. Embrace God's truth, love, and blessings He has in store for your life and your future!

In This Lifetime

"Sing the praises of the Lord, you his faithful people; praise his holy name. For his anger lasts only a moment, but his favor lasts a lifetime..."
(Psalm 30:4–5, NIV)

We have often heard that in life there is a season or time for everything. A time to plant and a time to harvest, a time to cry and a time to laugh, a time to this and a time to that. You may have heard a pastor say this is your season for grace and favor. I want to let you know every season is your season because God's mercy, grace, and favor does not know a season. We have to do our part by honoring the Word of God, obeying His commands, and walking in mercy and truth. By doing these things, we will find God's favor resting upon us. When we are accountable for our part, God will be accountable for His part.

Whatever you believe God for today, start proclaiming that shall come to pass. A turnaround in a relationship, a new job, a new house, a new car, improvement in your health, whatever it may be trusted and believe that God can and will do it in this lifetime!

Crawl to Walk to Run to Fly

"If anyone, then, knows the good they ought to do and doesn't do it; it is a sin for them." (James 4:17, NIV)

What do you think when you think of the voice of God? Do you hear a loud baritone voice that overpowers all other sounds? The Word tells us that God speaks in a small still voice, that soft, gentle voice in the back of your mind. That voice that tells you something is right or wrong, or if you should or shouldn't do something. That voice that we often call our conscience is the voice of God. Many times when that voice speaks to us, it is because we know what we should do, or how we should do it but we talk ourselves into what we want the answer to be. We make all types of excuses to justify our wrongdoings. We blame everyone but ourselves for the actions we perform.

God wants us to be accountable for our wrongdoings and our successes. He wants us to do it for our own sake to take ownership and trust in Him. By being accountable and trusting in God will cause God's blessings to begin to flow upon you. You have to build up your faith in the same way a baby learns to walk. You start by crawling, begin studying and meditating on God's Word. Stand and begin to walk. Remember you walk by faith not by sight, and in the beginning, you will stumble and fall a lot, but the more you work on it, the more stable you get. Run begin to be accountable for your actions, take ownership, and run towards the purpose and destiny God has ordained for your life. Fly like an eagle. When circumstances of life come up against you, fly above the storms and turbulence and let God guide you to safety.

Let Go

"Do not be misled: bad company corrupts good character."
(1 Corinthians 15:33, NIV)

Have you ever been in the presence of someone and just felt uncomfortable, or something about them just didn't sit well with your soul? Those very much so could be the Holy Spirit warning you this person is bad news. You may say I don't even know this person, but the spirit of God is saying this a major headache you want to avoid. This can also be applied to relationships; it is not always beneficial just to have a warm body next to you when that person's presence is killing your hopes, dreams, and aspirations. If you don't get rid of your bozo, how can God send you your Boaz?

God has given us free will to make our own decisions. So He will not force you to let go, but He will give you all the signs and warnings. Remember if God tells you to give something up, He has something bigger and better in the store waiting for you. As you grow and mature in Him you will see more clearly the paths He wants you to take. Your spirit of discernment grows stronger, and you find that letting go becomes easier. Bird of a feather flock together, we have all heard this saying. When you hang around individuals who are no good for you, you begin to act as they act and do as they do. Bad company can and will corrupt good character. Trust God's connections with the people in your life and let go of things that are not of His will and His way for your purposed destiny.

Big things come in small packages

"Whoever can be trusted with very little can also be trusted with much..."
(Luke 16:10, NIV)

When offered a choice of two gifts one being big and one being small, most people will take the larger gift because they think it has more or is of more value. With God, this is the furthest from the truth. God will give you little blessings that if you are humble enough to be appreciative of them will grow to be much larger blessings. We have to be a good steward of the pennies, nickels, and dime before we can handle bigger bills. We have to be grateful for a studio to be blessed with a mansion. Breath is often thought of like a little thing, and you don't consider it a big blessing, but when you can't breathe for even a second, you will realize how precious that blessing is. Be humble and thank God for the small prayers He may have answered, even if that prayer is that the sun shines and it does.

The Obedience begat Blessings

"If you fully obey the LORD your God and carefully follow all his commands I give you today, the LORD your God will set you high above all the nations on earth. All these blessings will come on you and accompany you if you obey the LORD your God." (Deuteronomy 28:1–2, NIV)

Those who faithfully seek after God find themselves receiving the rewards of God. When you follow His path for your life, there is a guarantee that there will be ups and downs, trials and tribulations, stormy days and sunny days, but those who endure the test receive great rest. When a runner races he starts out at a steady pace for he is prepared for the run ahead, as he nears the finish line his momentum increases and he pushes himself harder. We have to be that diligent with our race in life. As a child we paced ourselves with our faith, learning how to endure and building a foundation. Now as adults we have to go into a full out sprint on faith. Trusting and believing and in our obedience to God, no matter how hard it may seem, He will not only pull us through but will bless us during and after the storm. Always remember, when you obey God in the small, He will release big blessings. He has big opportunities, new levels of favor, healing, restoration, vindication, promotion, and more in your future. As you stay faithful to Him, you're going to step into the fullness of your destiny and be all that God has created you to be!

Harvest is Coming

"If you do these things, I will give you rains at the time they should come. The land will grow crops, and the trees of the field will grow their fruit." (Leviticus 26:4 NIV)

When things don't look sunny or are not flowing in the manner in which you would prefer it is so easy to get frustrated or aggravated. There are certain times when we must do certain things like plowing, seeding, watering, and nurturing. While we all would like for every season to be a season of reaping we have to put in the work. With the process we would not be ready and able to handle the blessings that God pours out on us. When we being to till the dirt is an example of when God is telling us the things we will have to deal with and move. We have to move some easy things, soil, and some hard things, rocks. Through each step in the process, God is preparing you for elevation and promotion.

If things are not moving as expeditiously as you would like, you have to be sure not to lose faith, hope, and sight of the end goal. Keep moving forward in drive and not slip into neutral or reverse. Keep a positive outlook and do what's right even in light of what might seem easy. God promises that your due season of harvest is coming and you have to believe and trust God in that. Be encouraged because your appointed time of increase, favor, and promotion is on its way, and He will fulfill every dream and desire He's placed within your heart.

"Instead of your shame you shall have double honor, and instead of confusion, they shall rejoice in their portion. Therefore in their land, they shall possess double; everlasting joy shall be theirs." (Isaiah 61:7, NIV)

Just as in this scripture have you ever gone through a dark period in your life? In this passage of scripture, the children of Israel were being held captive and being mistreated by other nations. To inspire them and give them encouragement and hope for a future God sent them this word. When the right time came, God stood true to His word. The same stands true for you. When you are at wit's end and just can't see your way through, God will send an encouraging word to lift your spirits and help you endure the fight.

The race isn't given to the swift, but to the one who endures to the end. Let this word bring encouragement to you as it did to the children of Israel; God will give to you as He did to Job, double for your trouble. He is the God of restoration; this means you will not get back what was taken from you, you will not be repaid for that which you have lost. This means God will go above and beyond to make the grass greener, the air clearer; it will be better than they had ever been before. Stand firm in faith and remain obedient to God's Word; you'll receive double for your trouble and see all His promises for your life come to pass!

All Things New

"He who was seated on the throne said, 'I am making everything new!'" (Revelation 21:5, NIV)

Do you recall when you first had that dream of something you wanted? Like a dream to be the best at a sport, advance in your career, be a dynamic parent, or even have a closer more personal relationship with God? When we begin something that we are passionate about we start out strong and at full speed ahead, then we hit stumbling blocks, and maybe things didn't progress as fast as you wanted. This is the point where people usually either give up or rather than keep forging forward they just settle for mediocrity.

God did not create you for mediocrity; He created you for greatness. When things don't work out immediately as we have planned that is when we must go back to the drawing board and begin again. Be like giant red oak and plant yourself firmly in the success that God has ordained and didn't stop until you reach that point. If you have given up on a dream or just stop dreaming, now is the time to go back and resurrect and dream again. Let God come in and make all things new. A new passion, new drive, new ambition, new beginning, it all starts with you having a new mindset on your success through your God.

Out With the Old In With the New New

"And no one pours new wine into old wineskins. Otherwise, the new wine will burst the skins; the wine will run out, and the wineskins will be ruined." (Luke 5:37, NIV)

Every year you see people post on social media and hear them say "New year, New me." I always wonder what exactly are they going to change if anything? You can't have the same negative things in your life and expect a positive outcome. You can say you are victorious with a defeated look on your face. You can't say you are more than a conqueror when you don't even try. Often time when you are trying to move forward toward your destiny you have to leave some baggage behind. That baggage could be friends, jobs, habits, and maybe even some family members. Old things will not always work with new methods. When you have a phone, and they release software updates, after so many updates your old phone doesn't function as good as it should. It's time for an upgrade.

You cannot live your future in your past, just as you can't drive forward looking in the rearview mirror. The things of your past were a lesson in preparation for your blessing. Things may have happened to you that you did not like, did not understand, may not have even been your fault, but you cannot allow those things to hold you in bondage. When new wine is poured into old wineskins, it will cause the old wineskins to burst. Your past cannot be poured into the new you because it will cause you to fail. Get a new new look at your life and what God has in store for you. Get a new new perspective on the blessings He has assigned to your hard and destined for your life. Get a new new look at you through the eyes of God. Start feeling good from your head to your shoes, praise God in advance for your new new life in Him. Don't wait until the new year for a new you; every day is a new opportunity for the new you to come out and be all that God has called you to be.

aith in God

"Moses reported this to the Israelites, but they did not listen to him because of their discouragement and harsh labor." (Exodus 6:9 NIV)

When a pastor, prophet, or anybody tells you that God has something better or bigger in store for you, do you believe them? Does it make your spirit jump with excitement? Do you receive their word? Being honest; there are times when what I see with my physical eyes and what I'm experiencing tells me bigger and better is impossible, instead of bigger and better it just gets by. The burdens of life and the adversity we often face time will place a damper on our spirits. You begin to focus more so on the negative than you do on the positive. You have to learn to sometimes tell yourself to shut up, be still and know that God is in control and listen to His voice. When we face hardships, we often talk ourselves out of our strength and endurance.

You were given two ears and one month; you should listen twice as much as you speak. This also applies to God; listen to His voice, twice as much as you speak. The Bible tells us to cast our cares on Him, give all our burdens to Him and take on His rest. When you say God I trust you to make a way, and you are following through on your part, God will show up and show out. When they thought you would fail, they will see your success. When they thought you wouldn't make it, they will see you in the first place. When they thought you would die, they will see you live and live life more abundantly. When things look dark and gloomy, rather than put yourself down, look to the hills from which comes your help. Know that God chose you and when you put your faith in God, He will bring you out not looking like what you've been through.

Time Recuperated

"I will repay you for the years the locusts have eaten— the great locust and the young locust, the other locusts and the locust swarm — my great army that I sent among you." (Joel 2:25, NIV)

Have you ever lost something? You search and search until you find it, and if you can't, you can easily get frustrated or discouraged. Sometimes, we feel the same way when it comes to life. When we spend time trying to build something or make something work, and it fails, we feel we have spent all that time for nothing and that is time lost. No, we cannot go back in time and recuperate that which is lost, but God can make the remaining time and your future so rewarding you don't even miss that time lost. You feel like that relationship you put you all into that went down the drain was a waste of your time, it was a lesson. It taught you something and made you a better person so that when you do come upon your soulmate, you are prepared to treat them like royalty and receive the royal treatment yourself.

You might have been on that job and have been giving it your all for years, but was always overlooked for the next level promotion. God can cause you to go from entry-level employee to mid-level manager or even cause you to start your own business that thrives beyond your dreams. When you trust in God, He will give back unto you all that you thought you had lost plus some. God will cause things to line up so that you can jump to where He wants you to be from your current situation. If you feel like I failed before why try again, you should because you serve the God of a second chance. He can make you change one thing, and it now works for your good. Keep the mindset I will recuperate what I lost, but it will be better than what was taken.

God said, "Challenge Accepted!"

"Now to him who can do immeasurably more than all we ask or imagine, according to his power that is at work within us," (Ephesians 3:20, NIV)

God said that He could do immeasurably more than all we ask or imagine. When have you asked God for something and not limited His powers? We ask God to bless us with an apartment when God wants to give you a house. You ask God for a job when He wants to give you a career or make you an entrepreneur. We have to stop asking God for little things and began to ask Him for great things. Yes keep asking for the small things, food, blessings, protection, wisdom, a closer walk with God, but also ask for those things you dream about. Ask for a successful business, ask for an award-winning book, ask for your dreams and desires, don't limit what God can do. There is that one thing you are praying for, something you desire that you alone can't accomplish, something that you can't complete by your own will and with your physical, psychological, and spiritual strength. That's what you challenge God with.

If you need scriptural confirmations just ask Joshua who prayed and asked God for more daylight, God accepted the challenge and the sun were stopped. Ask Elisha who prayed and asked God not to let it rain, God accepted the challenge, and for over three years there was not a drop of rain. They asked, stepped out on faith, God accepted and answered. Challenge God and see His hand move in your life with favor beyond measure.

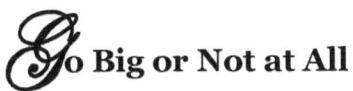o Big or Not at All

"You desire but do not have, so you kill. You covet but you cannot get what you want, so you quarrel and fight. <u>You do not have because you do not ask God.</u>" (James 4:2, NKJV)

You do not have because you do not ask. Many times we assume people know how we feel or know what we want. Sometimes, we are correct but often we are not. The same goes with God; He is not forceful, so He wants you to come to Him boldly with your desires. People will say well God is all powerful and all knowing; He knows what I want and what I need. As a human people know you need food but may not know what type of food you want. God knows you want a blessing but tell Him exactly what you desire. If you want a four bedroom three bathroom house, stop asking God for a two bedroom apartment. If you want to own your own business, stop asking God for a job. Ask God the true desires of your heart and let Him work out the details. Things in your life don't just happen; God orchestrated for them to line up in the exact order for your benefit. Don't limit God, rather let Him do what He wants to do, how He wants to do it in your life. Why ask for a little when He wants to give you a lot. Stand on your faith and go big or not at all.

Desires of Your Heart

"Take delight in the Lord, and he will give you the desires of your heart." (Psalm 37:4, NIV)

The songwriter wrote a song that said: "Oh Lord I love you, show me the desires of my heart." We all have desires or dreams that we hold deep in our hearts that we have not shared with anyone. We often think that these dreams are so big there is no way we can accomplish them. We do not have the manpower, or financial capability, or even the full layout of how it will work. He will place ideas or positions in front of you so big, and you tell yourself surely I do not have all the tools I need to succeed. There is a reason behind God's working in the manner; it causes us to trust Him and have faith that if He said it, it should come to pass. When we step out on faith, we are activating Gods super on our natural. We are giving Him the okay and the clearance to do what He needs to and can do in our lives. We are saying God I yield to your will and your way, I may not understand, and I may not see, but I believe you will do it. If you are in a place where you feel you are in a holding pattern and awaiting clearance to land, just trust in God that the runway is being cleared and all the desires of your heart will come to pass. God made you a promise, and He will bring to pass that which He has promised. Pray, meditate, praise, worship, and give Him free reign to give you the desires of your heart.

igher

"The Lord says, "My thoughts are not like yours. Your ways are not like mine." (Isaiah 55:8, ERV)

We all have things that we desire of God, from dreams we want to achieve things only He can turn around in our favor, but too often we make a great God into a small God. We placed limits on what He can do by us giving Him directions and not letting Him take the wheel. We want Him only to use certain things and people who we have deemed the right ones versus letting Him cross our paths with the chosen ones. We map it all out in our heads, and things have to flow in the manner which we have set. We have to be fluid and able to change the plan as God sees fit.

What you want in a day God may say takes a week, but in that time it will be stable and successful, not frail and fail. The Clark Sisters had a song which they said "Higher," we have to think higher, look higher, praise higher, and walk higher. God is higher than anything we will ever face and endure. When we see things as He sees them what we thought was big and bad, turns out to be small and easy. You have to keep an open mind to say I will trust that God will work this out in my favor if I am patient and keep the faith. Surrender your will and your way to Him, trust in Him, believe in Him, know that He has your back, and His goal and desire is to take you Higher.

Close to Open

"I know what you do. I have put before you an open door that no one can close. I know you are weak, but you have followed my teaching. You were not afraid to speak my name." (Revelation 3:8, ERV)

Michelle Williams said during a performance "When Jesus opens a door, it's a door that no man close" she follows it to say "Do you believe that tonight?" That question stands true do you believe that in your life? Sometimes when God closes a door, we get upset and question why did He do that. You feel that person or situation may not have been the best but it was working and you were okay with that. We have to realize that when God shuts a door, He opens another that has bigger, better, and greater in store for us. We may see a rational opportunity, but just because it's rational to us, doesn't mean that it's the way God wants it done. Let go of your agenda and walk in faith with God's agenda. Let God open and close the necessary doors to get you to your destiny. Let go and let God! When you close, He will open!

The Promise

"Then the word of the Lord came to Elijah: 'Leave here, turn eastward and hide in the Kerith Ravine, east of the Jordan. You will drink from the brook, and I have directed the ravens to supply you with food there. " (1 Kings 17:2–4, NIV)

When baking a cake, you have to follow the directions in the exact order if you want to get a successful result. You can't mix the flour and egg then bake and expect the cake to taste good or even look good. The same goes for the directions that God gives us. Yes, He wants to bless us and give us the desires of our heart, but we have to follow His directions to get to the promise. In this passage of text God gave Elijah specific instructions, the only disclaimer was that he had to obey and follow God's plan to walk into his promise. God lines up the right connections, people, and opportunities to help you get to your promised destiny. We have to do our part and stay connected to God's word, keep the faith, keep praise on our lips, and when the going gets tough, we have to keep going. Follow the Godly road, and you will make it to your promise.

I Will Remain Confident in This.....

"I remain confident of this: I will see the goodness of the Lord in the land of the living." (Psalm 27:13, NIV)

Is everything in your life perfect, and be honest? In the Bible, David had seen some good days, but at this moment he was going through an extremely tough time in his life. Everything that could go wrong was going wrong. Everybody can relate to having that feeling at some point in life. When life throws you a lemon, you have to make a lemon meringue pie, lemon pepper wings, lemon pound cake, and lemonade. When life gets hard you praise harder, let the enemy know when he gets big your God is bigger. What you put your focus on is what you will begin to see transpire in your life. Focus on the good, and you will see good, focus on the negative and you will see the negative. See what you desire and desire what you see. Remain confident in this you will see the goodness of the Lord while you are living!

 Lifted

"He lifted me out of the grave. He lifted me from that muddy place. He picked me up, put me on solid ground, and kept my feet from slipping." (Psalm 40:2, ERV)

We have often heard of having a valley experience, but have you ever had a pit experience? That time when you feel disappointment, depression, frustration, anger, hopelessness, fear, or you just can't see your way. You have to remember even in our darkest hour God is still with us. It's like the footprint poem when we think we are walking alone that is when God is carrying us. When you can't see a way out, you have to remember God has the master plan and have already made a way; you have just to trust and believe.

God never does anything without it having a purpose and a reason for your life. Everything we endure teaches us a lesson that prepares us for our blessing. No matter how you ended up in the situation you are in be it by your own hands or the hands of the others, God still will make it work for your good. You may experience discomfort at times, but discomfort makes us move so that God can get us where He wants us to be. Shake of your negative thoughts, actions, and mindset, look at yourself through God's eyes. When the storm rages see it as the soil being watered versus life tossing you. Trust that God is preparing you for something greater. He will keep you lifted in the midst of the storm.

He will Hide You

"In the day of trouble he will keep me safe in his dwelling; he will hide me in the shelter of his sacred tent and set me high upon a rock."
(Psalm 27:5, NIV)

When we see homeless people in the streets, a natural disaster, or a mass killing people often question where God is in these events. In the same manner when we are going through catastrophic events or just hardships we ask where is God and why would He allow this to happen. In all truths, I cannot give you an answer as to why He allows these things to happen, but I can say we have to trust Him still as hard as that may be. We have to trust that He knows we are in pain and we are in a vulnerable questioning place, but also still trust that He is there offering His comfort and peace to our vexed hearts and minds.

He feels our pain and has a plan for us to see the silver lining in that dark cloud. That lining could be law reform, new residence, new job, a new partner, even a new you. The devil has one job that is threefold, that is to kill, steal, and destroy. He wants to kill your dreams and ambition, steal your peace and joy, and destroy your faith. While the devil may not directly attack you, he utilizes situations and circumstances to take your eyes and focus off Jesus. When Peter took his eyes off Jesus, he begins to sink. When we take our eyes off Jesus, we too begin to sink, but just as Jesus was there for Peter, He is there for us.

In the times of trouble know that God is in your corner and is there for you. He will hide you in his safe place and raise that standard against the adversary. Trust that in all the calamity and chaos, in all that we do not understand or agree with, God has a master plan, and in some way, shape, form, and fashion it will work out for our good.

Tell God Your Desires

"Do not be afraid, little flock, for your Father has been pleased to give you the kingdom." (Luke 12:32, NIV)

My friend, you are a child of the King, you are a prince or princess, and you are royalty! As with any parent God wants to bless you and see you live a happy, joyful life. He wants to give you the desires of your heart that will keep you smiling and giving Him glory, honor, and praise. Our rewards are not just freely given. Like getting a degree, you have to put in some work, and it is earned. The work we have to put in to see our blessings flow are similar to obtaining a degree. You have to be persistent, study, and show yourself approved. You have to stand firm in your work and your faith. If you wavier like a leaf in the wind, you will be blown away.

However, if you stand anchored in the foundation on that is Christ and following His direction, you will stand the test, pass the test, and find yourself abundantly blessed. Don't ever be afraid to go to your father, the King, with your petitions. It's being Him delight and joy to grant you your wishes, but you have to make your request known. Come to him boldly standing on the foundation of your faith and knowing that He loves you and wants to bless you in abundance. Tell God your desires, stand on your faith, and watch your life grow and prosper.

Let it Go

"And when you stand to pray, if you hold anything against anyone, forgive them, so that your Father in heaven may forgive you your sins."
(Mark 11:25, NIV)

Everybody at some point and time in life has been hurt, offended, betrayed, lied on, talked about, and mistreated. Sometimes life is like a paper cut, it hurts and is painful, but it heals quickly with no scar. Other times life is like a deep cut, it is excruciating and takes time to heal and leaves behind a reminder that it was there. Whatever the injury life throws at you be it a paper cut or wound, you have to begin the healing process. That includes forgiving the person that inflicted the injury, even if that person is you. It is hardest for us to forgive ourselves than it is to forgive others at times. We remind ourselves of our failures and disappointments. You have to forgive to begin the healing process. Forgiveness releases the bondage that was holding us captive to the situation. Yes, the injury was wrong, we are not condoning it, but we are growing and becoming stronger from it. Once we have forgiven the injurer, let it go, let it go, let it go. Stop running back to that wound and reopening it. Do not continue to torture yourself, find that light at the end of the tunnel and shine it throughout the entire tunnel. In the darkness things hide that try to tear you down, but in the light, you can see clearly and fight it off. Let it go; it cannot hold you back anymore, let it go and let God handle it.

It Could be an Angel

"how God anointed Jesus of Nazareth with the Holy Spirit and power, and how he went around doing good and healing all who were under the power of the devil because God was with him." (Acts 10:38, NIV)

A lot of people associate Jesus with the many miracles and teachings He did among the multitude. Yes, his miracles were great and wonderful, but often time we forget the first real miracle Jesus did. Many people would not even consider it a miracle, but it is something we all can do. Before Jesus did anything, He was nice and good to the people. So many times we overlook individuals who do not look like us, act like us, or believe like us. We have to do as Jesus did and still show hospitality to these individuals, they could be an angel in disguise.

When you show hospitality people take notice and become curious as to what makes you so happy and generous with your kindness. This inquiry makes them want to know who it is that gives you this peace and joy. God tells us to let our light shine before men, let your goodness and kindness shown to the masses. Let them see your strength and endurance in the time of struggle. The Word continues to say that they may glorify your God in Heaven, this will make them want to serve the God that preserves you. Remember every trial and tribulation you go through; every test is just a testimony. Tell your testimony and be good to everyone you see, you never know you could be entertaining an angel in disguise.

Be a Blessing

"But since you excel in everything — in faith, in speech, in knowledge, in complete earnestness and in the love we have kindled in you — see that you also excel in this grace of giving."
(2 Corinthians 8:7, NIV)

In this scripture, we are told that we excel in our faith, speech, knowledge, earnestness, and love. While this is great, we are also told to make sure we excel in giving. So often when we are blessed, we want to hold the blessing to ourselves. We become selfish with what God has poured out on us. If we are to excel, we have to learn how to be a blessing when we are blessed. No, I am not saying that when you are blessed with a good amount of money give it all away, but sow into another person's life the way God sowed into your life. If you know of job openings, refer people to apply, if you know a scholarship that's available tell a potential student.

We have all heard the saying it is better to give than to receive. I enjoy giving the gift of hope to people. That can be done with a simple smile, or a yes you can achieve that dream or even a hug. I enjoy when someone asks for prayer, it gives me yet another reason to go to the throne of God and have a conversation with Him. Giving is not always financial, but you can give hope, courage, wisdom, love, even peace. When people see you as a giver, then they know you serve a giving God. When you walk in the ministry of God, you will find your life blessed and blessed abundantly. Don't just be blessed daily, but be a blessing daily.

The One Protection

*"Because he loves me,' says the LORD, 'I will rescue him; I will protect him, for he acknowledges my name." *(Psalm 91:14, NIV)

When you are a believer in the power and authority of God, you will find protection when you did not even know you had or needed it. Walking down the street, you could be a victim of a senseless crime, driving in your car you could be in a serious accident. These are the easier way to identify things that God protects us from. Many times we don't see how He protects us from people who are trying to take from us, under the disguise of benefiting us. We all have come across that one person who is always your friend when they are in need, and you can provide. People in your life to drain all your energy, put down your hopes, turn your beautiful dreams into horrific nightmares.

People who are always negative or find a reason to complain about everything. God protects us from these people, but we have to activate the protection. Alarm systems do not work unless they are activated. You have to activate God by allowing Him to give you that discernment and trusting when He says no, or leave, to leave it at no and leave, no ifs, and, or buts about it. When God tells you to move trust Him and just move, it could very well be your life or death situation. Remember because God loves you, He will rescue you when you make mistakes and fall short. When you are in danger He will protect you and guide you into the safety of his arms. You have to just rely on the one protection system that always works in your favor.

Look Where He's Brought You From

"Remember what the Lord your God did to Miriam along the way after you came out of Egypt." (Deuteronomy 24:9, NIV)

When you tell people where God has brought you from you are doing two things. One you are giving your testimony and bragging about how good God has been and is being to you. Two you are giving that person hope that whatever they are going through, God will bring them out as He did to you. The good thing about our God is that He loves when you speak of His goodness, grace, and mercy.

He loves when you tell others how you got over that mountain, how He made a way out of no way. You may think oh well he just gave me bread to eat, but to someone who is hungry, to him providing bread is like a full five-course meal. You were in that abusive relationship and God delivered you out. You may have been battered and beaten, but you still have a life. That will help someone who is currently in that situation know that God can deliver them as well.

You were molested as a child, or a tragic event happened, yes it was bad, yes it was wrong, yes it hurts, but you survived, and you have to allow it to make you stronger. Your testimony can let someone know that you can grow and be successful in spite of the hell you have been through. The older church mothers would say "When I look back over my life and all the things God has brought me through." You have to look back over your life and see where you have come.

You might not be where you want to be, but you are not where you use to be. We are so quick to remember the things that did not work, our failures, disappointments, defeats, instead remember your attempts, your small steps, your successes, your achievements, look at how far you have come even if it is just a small step. Celebrate one day of not smoking, then one week, then one month, before long you will find yourself celebrating years of tobacco free.

I employ you to look where He's brought you from. Tell everyone you meet, I've been through the fire and I've been through the flood. But I don't smell like smoke, and I have the best flood insurance provider Jesus.

reat God

"I will never forget your precepts, for by them you have preserved my life."
(Psalm 119:93, NIV)

Where would I be if it had not been for the Lord on my side? We all have done things that should have ended our lives. Things that should have taken us out of here, it was the grace of God that kept us and is still keeping us. We hear God telling us to go right, and we go left anyway just to see if our way is better than the way He told us. We are humans, and we make mistakes, it's the truth. We can go to school and get all the degrees in the world; we can hit the gym and be able to bench press fifty thousand pounds easily. It is still no match for the wisdom and strength of God. God has the innate ability to open doors we cannot and could not open for ourselves.

God causes the right people to cross our paths and see not only what we already possess, but also see our potential, and gives us the extra we need to be where God wants us to be. Always give thanks for the good, bad, ugly, and indifferent. Always give thanks for the good, bad, ugly, and indifferent. Remember when praises go up, great bountiful blessings come down. God is worthy of all glory, honor, and praise when you give Him all glory, honor, and praise you will see how great He is in your life. You will see that you lack nothing, want for nothing, and have peace that passes even your understanding, joy that overflows so much that others get joy. You will find your future has great things in store for you from a great God.

ll Things

"In all your ways acknowledge Him, and He shall direct your paths."
(Proverbs 3:6, NIV)

God is always with us, in our good time and our bad. When we want Him there, and even when we want Him gone, He is always there. Many times we ask God for an answer, but because we have already come up with the answer that works for us, we ignore God's true answer, or brush it off. What we have to understand is that God seeks to help us in everything in life. Everything from the little things, what color socks to wear, to the big things which should I marry. God wants to be in it all. The only thing stopping Him is you. God will only do as much as you will allow Him to do. He is gentle and not forceful, so He will give you the option to do what right, or let you do what you want to do. We can't just invite Him in on Sunday when we attend service.

Yes, He loves when we worship together and strengthens one another, but He is also worthy of the praise Monday through Saturday. Don't just seek His input on the major decisions in life, but learn to allow Him to guide every decision. This passage tells us in all our ways acknowledge God. Again the Bible is very specific in the words it chose. It did not say in some of your ways, in a few of your ways, in as often as you like, no it said in all your ways acknowledge Him. By doing this, you will find He will direct your paths and you will find the road easier to travel. Letting Him direct your paths you will find when you run into a mountain; you will have everything you need to move that mountain and keep moving forward. Acknowledge God in ALL things, and He will bless you in ALL things.

Seek Help

"The people of Judah came together to seek help from the Lord; indeed, they came from every town in Judah to seek him. " (2 Chronicles 20:4, NIV)

For God to step in and begin to do what only He can do in your life, you must first seek Him. You have to acknowledge that He is all powerful and all sovereign. By acknowledging His power and seeking Him you can ask Him for guidance, direction, and help. The good thing about God is nothing is too small to ask for, and nothing is too big. From God, please help me find my keys, to God please help me maintain my sanity, God can handle it. We have to step out on faith and trust in God. Trust is the foundation of any relationship, and this is inclusive of our relationship with God. If you do not trust Him how can you trust and believe that He will come to your aid and rescue. Sure somethings you can do on your like picking out your socks or finding your keys. But when you learn to hear His voice in the little things you will find it a whole lot easier to hear His voice in the big things. What should have been stressful and a struggle won't bother you near as much. You will find His anointing resting on you giving you peace in the midst of all the chaos. Ask God for help and let Him be your present help in all aspects of your life.

He Will Keep You

"I will go before you and will level the mountains; I will break down gates of bronze and cut through bars of iron." (Isaiah 45:2 NIV)

When you keep God first in your life, He said He would go before you and level the mountains. That means the areas in your life that will cause you pain, struggle, turmoil, heartache, and hardship God will level them. Things that to you will seem like Mount Everest will only be the start of an ant hill. He will break down the gates of bronze that are holding you back from achieving your goals and dreams. The things that are blocking you like iron from moving forward He will cut through them. When we stay true to the being that God created us to be, acknowledge Him in all aspects of our life we will see how God manifest Himself in our future before we dream of it.

We will find where most businesses close, or writer's block to set it, or finances begin to decrease, health begins to fail, stress and worry begin to overtake us; God is already there with the answer. That storm that you saw raging and wave that is causing you fear God has already said peace be still and it was still. When we are in need of something should not be the only time we acknowlege God, He should always be on your mind. Be dedicated and determined to make your relationship with God your highest priority. Keep Him first in all that you do, and He will go before you and level your mountains, breakdown bronze gates, and cut through bars of iron. He will keep you if you keep Him first.

ray Continually

"Pray continually," (1 Thessalonians 5:17, NIV)

To pray we do not have to be on our knees with our eyes closed and head bowed. Pray is a state of mind, it's an attitude that you pose and take on. When you are thinking about God, or talking to God, or praising God, or worshiping God, you are in prayer. Prayer is our communication with God. It is not only just our verbal actions, but prayer is also non-verbal. God hears every tear; every hand lifted up, every thought He hears what we do not say aloud. Develop the habit of always acknowledging, talking to, praising, and worshiping Him. That's when you will see God step in and fight all of your battles. Be determined to pray continually. Remember that God is not only with you, but also for you, and when you acknowledge Him in all your ways, He will direct your paths.

With Him

"I am the vine; you are the branches. If you remain in me and I in you, you will bear much fruit; apart from me you can do nothing." (John 15:5, NIV)

Jesus has to be the roots of your tree of life. A tree cannot survive without its roots. It's rooted not only give it stability, but it also provides nutrients from the soil so that the tree can bear fruit. Without the support and food, the roots provide the tree will die and easily be taken down the forces that come against it. This applies to Jesus in our lives. If we do not allow Him to be our roots, we will easily succumb to the principalities that are working against us. If we do not allow Him to supply what we need, then we will not bear good fruit. To grow tall and strong we have to plant ourselves into the Word of God.

We have to acknowledge that without Him we cannot accomplish anything. God orchestrates everything in our lives from our first to our last breaths. Therefore, He knows the storms that will come and cause you to bend, maybe even become level to the ground, but you won't break. By staying connected and anchored in Him you will see that everything you went through, in some way, made you a stronger person. When you are connected to Him the fruit you shall bare will not only bless you, but it will be a blessing and a seed in someone else life. You will find yourself not only being blessed but also a blessing to others. Without Him there is no life, With Him, there is no limit.

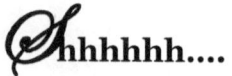hhhhhh....

"He says, "Be still, and know that I am God; I will be exalted among the nations, I will be exalted in the earth." (Psalm 46:10, NIV)

Everything and everybody are in a hurry nowadays. We put so much on our plate to the point it feels more like a platter. We try to make 36 hours out of 24 with the hustle and bustle of what we call life. God calls us to be still and knows that He is God. This means He wants us to take a break and just rest and enjoy the peace that only He gives. He wants us to be still and silent so that we can hear His voice and His plans for our lives. His plan that makes everything we desire come easier and are a whole lot less stressful. He wants us to move at the speed of God and not the speed of man. Daily take time to study and meditate on the Word of God.

Make time daily to praise and exalt His name. Make time to glorify Him for the things He has done, is doing, and will do. In that same manner, thank Him for the things He has not done and will not do. Remember delayed does not mean denied, and something you think might be good for you in reality are not. Take time every day to stop with everything and give God some time to talk to you. Let Him fill your day with His love and grace, let Him speak to your heart and mind, seek His peace and He will give you His joy.

Obey Your Thirst

"but whoever drinks the water I give them will never thirst. Indeed, the water I give them will become in them a spring of water welling up to eternal life." (John 4:14, NIV)

About 71% of the Earth is covered in water. About 60% of the human body is made of water. Every living being, plant and animal alike, need water to survive. When we are outside on hot days or enjoying life and building up a sweat, our bodies need even more water to maintain its health and functionality. In that same manner, we have to drink the water of life from God. We have to water the seed He planted in us with His Word for it to grow. By refreshing our mind, as well as our heart, we allow God to heal those things that have been causing us pain and turmoil. We allow Him to nurture us when we feel brokenhearted, alone, sad, and depressed.

When we drink from Him, He said we would never thirst again. That means when we take Him into us He renews Himself with every praise, worship, prayer, and study of His word. The thirst that we have for greatness, He can fulfill. The thirst for a successful business, partnership, career, health, abundance, He is the only one that can quench it. Go to God and receive His refreshing water of life, in it, you will find peace and joy that only God can give. Obey your thirst, drink of Christ.

emember God

"Then those who feared the LORD talked with each other, and the LORD listened and heard. A scroll of remembrance was written in his presence concerning those who feared the LORD and honored his name."
(Malachi 3:16, NIV)

We remember the things that we hold dear to our heart: your first kiss, your baby first steps, graduation, completion of your book, among many other things. We do this because it brought us happiness and joy. In that same manner, when we worship and praise God, He holds that dear to His heart and that brings Him joy and happiness. Every time you talk about God to anyone or even to yourself, he takes note. Every time you praise or thank Him, He takes note. These are not just like notes that are placed in a storage locker somewhere never to be seen again. No these are kept before God to constantly remind Him of those that are thinking about Him. How does it feel to know that the creator of the heaven and the earth love when you think about Him? When a person is on your mind you check on them, see if they are okay and if you can help with anything. God does the same thing! When you are thinking of Him, He checks in with you to see if you are okay, if you need anything, and then He begins to bless you with those things. All day and every day keep God on your mind, always thanking Him, remembering His promises, standing on His word. When you remember God, God will remember you.

ait

"For the revelation awaits an appointed time; it speaks of the end and will not prove false. Though it lingers, wait for it; it will certainly come and will not delay." (Habakkuk 2:3, NIV)

Wait for a word many of us are not a fan of. Our society has been geared to want things instantly. Gone are the days when you would: pick the greens, wash and clean them, cut them, boil the water, add your seasonings, then cook the greens. Now we open a can, heat, and eat. With God, we ask Him for things and expect an instant answer or instant provisions. We ask God to heal our health, but don't want to wait for the healing. If we are diligent in our seeking of God, we will see and understand His plan. You have to be patient your increase is coming, your healing is coming, your promotion is coming, your breakthrough is coming, there is a shift, and it is in your favor. God's promise will be fulfilled in you and through you if you are patient!

Delayed does not mean denied! While you are waiting to get ready for what God Is about to bless you with. He said that everything He has destined for your life has to come to fruition, it will not prove false. That means this struggle will not last always, the season of lack will end, you will be above and not beneath. When we wait on God, He not only gives us what He promised but He gives us interest for the waiting period. We will find ourselves happier, achieving more, being more productive, and accomplishing things we didn't think we could. When we are firm in our standing on faith, dedicated to the Word of God, and patiently waiting on God to fulfill His promises we will see Him move just like that. The key is to be patient and wait.

His Grace is Sufficient

"But he said to me, "My grace is sufficient for you, for my power is made perfect in weakness." Therefore I will boast all the more gladly about my weaknesses, so that Christ's power may rest on me."
(2 Corinthians 12:9, ESV)

In life, we all have areas where we can improve, or we could be better in. Instead of beating yourself up and putting yourself down, go to God who will give you His strength. You have to have a humble spirit and admit that alone you cannot accomplish anything, but with God, on your side, you can accomplish everything. We often think that when we are weak, we are not able to defeat the giant in front of us. It's when we are at our weakest; God is at His strongest. We have to learn to step aside, let go of our ego and pride when we stop trying to figure it out on our own, that's when God shows up the strongest. When we constantly interfere with what God is doing it gives the impression that we have it all under control and don't need Him. That's when He steps back and allows us to make those mistakes. Stop letting things hold you back and in bondage in life. His grace is sufficient for you; all thing are working for your good.

Who God Rewards

"And without faith, it is impossible to please God because anyone who comes to him must believe that he exists and that he rewards those who earnestly seek him." (Hebrews 11:6, NIV)

A house built with no foundation cannot stand against the elements of nature. The same is true for a person who desires of God but does not stand on faith. Doing something in a routine does not guarantee success. If you play the lottery every day consistently for a year does not guarantee you will ever win the big prize. Going to church every Sunday and Wednesday but not acting on faith or standing on faith does not guarantee what you desire of the Lord will come to you. The Word tells us without faith it is impossible to please God. It's like expecting a check from a job you don't work. God says He blessed anyone!

Anyone being: Black, White, Latino, Asian, tall, short. Skinny, fat, straight, gay, anyone with breath basically, but they must believe that He exists. Also, they must earnestly seek Him. Seek Him in the good when there is a smile on your face. Seek Him in the bad when it seems like you are about to lose your mind. When you seek Him those things which seemed impossible become possible. That which seemed difficult becomes easier. That which seemed unobtainable becomes obtainable. Build your faith to know that by my faith mountains will move and rivers will flow, meaning hardships are moved, and blessings abound.

Praise is What I Do

"Remind the people to be subject to rulers and authorities, to be obedient, to be ready to do whatever is good," (Titus 3:1, NIV)

How do you show honor to God? Is it by going to church every Sunday and Wednesday? By participating in praise and worship? Is it by reading a daily devotional to give you a bit of inspiration? Yes, there are great ways to intentionally honor God, but did you know there are ways you do it unintentionally? In our society, today actions speak volumes over words. People see what you do and judge you off of that versus the words that you speak. You say you are a prompt person but church starts at noon, and you arrive weekly fifteen minutes late. People look at your lifestyle and if it is one that they hold in high regards will want to know how you are living and what makes you so happy.

When your entire being gives God praise, it raises eyebrows. When they talk about you, and you never let it deter your smile, people will wonder why are you still having joy. When they try to break you down, yet you stand tall, they will want to know who is keeping you up. When you stare death in the face and decide I shall live, people will want to know where your strength and help come from. We have to set the standard of what people should see and expect in and of life. Your reputation, character, and spirit should speak of you before you ever arrive, and it should make people want to know your God. Do what you know is good so that people will want to serve your God. Let people know in spite of wrong; I will do right for praise is what I do.

ree to Win

"I am the Living One; I was dead, and now look, I am alive forever and ever! And I hold the keys of death and Hades." (Revelation 1:18, NIV)

Picture if you are in a hurry to get to work. You grab your briefcase, your coffee, and your coat. You turn the lock on the front door, walk out to the car, place the items in your hands on top of the car, go to grab your keys to unlock the car only to realize the keys are in the house on the counter. Maybe you got out of the lock and pressed the lock button on the door, and your keys are laying on the seat. Have you ever tried to unlock a door and the key went into the lock but didn't open the door because it was the wrong key? Not having the proper keys can be a rather frustrating and upsetting situation. It causes you to lose time, energy and can darken the mood of your entire attitude and day.

On a spiritual level, we need the keys to open the doors of blessings God has for us in our life. We don't have to stand outside and be trapped by the elements of the principalities that are working against us. We don't have to succumb to the vicissitude of life. We don't have to stay chained and bound by the events of our past. God has taken back the keys to every stronghold in our lives and given us the power to request those keys and be set free. If you feel defeated, sick, depressed, mediocre, or holding yourself by events of your past, break free. Call on the name of Jesus and ask Him to free you from all that is holding you back. Call on Him and receive your hope, joy, and your freedom. He paid the price for your sins, now get free and win.

disAPPOINTED

"For such people are not serving our Lord Christ, but their own appetites. By smooth talk and flattery, they deceive the minds of naive people." (Romans 6:18, NIV)

September 22, 1862, President Abraham Lincoln signed the Emancipation Proclamation declaring all slaves free. It wasn't until June 19, 1865, that the announcement came to Galveston, Texas that the proclamation had gone forth of the abolition of slavery. For almost three years people were free but didn't know they were free. Their freedom was held captive by the masters who wanted to maintain control over their lives in its entirety.

The slaves, who through the Christian religion, knew Christ appointed them for something, but this couldn't be it. A slave by the name of Bridget "Biddy" Mason was born on a Hancock, Georgia plantation. She was given as a wedding gift and moved to Logtown, Mississippi. Beaten, deprived of education, and raped, she bore three children by her slave master. With the way life was she was disappointed. In your life things may have happened, things went wrong, you were beaten or raped physically, mentally, spiritually, or all the above. It seemed as if you could not see your way before something else came blocking your vision.

Just when Bridget was disappointed, God stepped in and said Didn't I Say APPOINTED! Bridget went on to found the First African Methodist Episcopal Church in Los Angeles, California. Upon at her passing in 1891, she had a net-worth of $300,000, equivalent to $8,306,687.28 in today's market. God took her disappointments and showed her how, through it all: the ups and downs, good and bad, happy and sad, He appointed her.

She went from rags to riches. God is now seeking to do the same with you and in your life. He knows the hardships; He knows the pain, He knows: your trials and tribulations, He knows your struggles, He knows your disappointments, but He said YOU ARE appointed! You are appointed above, and not beneath, you are appointed the head and not the tail, you are appointed more than a conqueror and not just a conqueror, you are appointed the lender and not the borrower, you are appointed free and not in slavery bound by anything. Where you feel disAPPOINTED, remember God says **"Didn't I Say APPOINTED!"**

www.ingramcontent.com/pod-product-compliance
Lightning Source LLC
Chambersburg PA
CBHW032125090426
42743CB00007B/473